COOKERY
FOR
absolute
BEGINNERS

ABOUT THE AUTHOR

Lynette Baxter gained a degree in Home Economics from the University of Surrey, which led to a career in the food industry. She works on product and recipe development for major high street retailers, with a particular interest in introducing exciting new flavours from around the world. She has a firm belief that anyone can cook anything armed with a good recipe and hopes that this book will encourage others to feel the same.

COOKERY
FOR
absolute
BEGINNERS

Lynette Baxter

ACKNOWLEDGEMENTS

Design: Amanda Hawkes
Illustrations: Lesley Cullen
Cover photograph: Colin Taylor Productions
Editor: Nicola Baxter

The author and publishers wish to thank
Annie Forsberg, Bernadette Newman,
Jill Parkinson, Sue Poulter and Adrian Reeve
for their help with this book.

This edition first published by Abbeyville Press
an imprint of Bookmart Limited
Registered Number 2372865
Trading as Bookmart Limited, Desford Road, Enderby,
Leicester, LE9 5AD, England

Produced for Bookmart Limited by Nicola Baxter

Printed in Great Britain

CONTENTS

YOU CAN COOK!

It is a daunting moment when an inner grumbling tells you food is required and the realisation dawns that nobody but yourself is going to provide it. Several options spring to mind – casually calling in on friends in a hopeful manner, a swift trip to the chip shop or resorting to a large packet of chocolate digestives. But clearly, since you are clasping this book, there is a fourth choice.

There is nothing particularly clever or mysterious about cooking, but there can be much more to it than quashing a pang of hunger. It should be a pleasure. True, if you are daily rushing home from a hard day's work to feed a family, the fun may sometimes be a little difficult to find, but food has a great capacity for bringing people together and the ability to cook, for yourself and others, can grow into a lifelong pleasure.

In writing this book, I have had to make some assumptions about you! Perhaps you are living away from home for the first time, in your new flat, or just beginning college. Maybe your circumstances have changed and you have to cook for yourself for the first time. The equipment you have and the type of kitchen in which it is to be used will be affected by your circumstances.

Although it is several years ago, I can still vividly remember my first day at college and the sight of the little worktop oven with two hot plates that graced the kitchen of my hall of residence. This, and the domestic-sized refrigerator, were designed to serve fourteen of us. As I was already an enthusiastic cook, this was a daunting prospect, but it is amazing how many meals can be produced in a single pan, and several cherished recipes of those years have lived on to appear in this book. Adapt yourself to the available equipment. If your cooker door has to be propped shut with a rolling pin – things didn't improve much when I moved into a flat – put your soufflé-making on hold.

Some pieces of equipment *are* essential and these are discussed in more detail later (pages 9–20). The list beginning on page 19 contains all the equipment you require to make any of the basic recipes in this book. Of course, if you are the proud possessor of a food processor or a microwave oven, or even a brand new kitchen bursting with equipment, that is a bonus!

Quite often, new cooks are on a tight budget. It is tempting, especially if cooking for one, to buy ready-made recipe dishes. Since a manufacturer and supermarket have already made fairly sizeable profits on these, they are probably more expensive than cooking something yourself, but sometimes they make a quick and easy treat. It may seem better to buy larger packets of ingredients because they tend to be cheaper, gram for gram, but you will have to consider both your storage space and how quickly you will use particular items. Pages 21–52 give more details of what I would consider to be basic standbys for the store-cupboard, but you will, of course, have your own favourite ingredients too. Many of the recipes in this book consist of a basic recipe that should be economical to make, followed by variations, which may include more exotic ingredients.

One of the most positive things to have happened recently is the growth of cookery programmes on television and radio, on which a whole host of enthusiastic cooks really encourage one to "have a go". On the other hand, some gourmet cookery programmes can plummet one to the depths of despair, as a supercook whips up a three-course meal in half an hour. Refuse to be intimidated by these people! Admire what they do and let it inspire you to further forays into the kitchen, where you will soon realise that things need not be so difficult. Cookery, like so many other skills, involves grasping the basics and then launching forth. Once you have mastered the initial stages, literally a whole world of recipes is open to you. Armed with a good cookery book, you should not need to make major mistakes. True, we all have our minor disasters – a lumpy sauce, a sausage that is charcoal on the outside and raw in the middle, a batch of biscuits that weld themselves to the baking tray, but most problems can be overcome, disguised or turned into something completely different!

When you first read a cookery book, it can seem as though it is written in a foreign language. What is creaming, basting, braising, folding, rubbing-in or marinating? How do you grease and line a cake tin, finely chop an onion or skin a tomato? Why do you preheat an oven, seal a piece of meat or "rest" pastry? This book explains the above terms and many more. It will give tips and tricks to make certain tasks easier and provide variations to extend your basic repertoire much further. But its main aim is to give you an enthusiasm for cooking that will last a lifetime and act as the springboard for many future culinary triumphs.

USING THIS BOOK

THE RECIPES

One way of presenting a cookery book for beginners is to offer perhaps ten menus, each one giving exact shopping lists and time plans to ensure that the meal turns out exactly as intended. Another is to concentrate on basic recipes: pastry, sponges, sauces and so forth. The first type is fine in its way – you can produce ten splendid meals but nothing else. The second kind is frankly boring – you want to produce substantial food, not the perfect egg custard. Instead, I have collected together a selection of favourite recipes that are simple and straightforward to make. They will provide you with satisfactory results straightaway and enable you to move on to more advanced cookery books.

With any new piece of equipment, you are always advised to read the instructions carefully before using it. A cookery book is no exception. Take time to read through the opening chapters of this book, rather than plunging straight into a recipe – you will find that it is time well spent. There are a few things to consider before you begin to prepare food.

EQUIPMENT

Some basic equipment is obviously essential. I have listed what I believe to be the minimum utensils you will need to make any of the recipes in this book, but it is also worth considering more sophisticated equipment for when your enthusiasm is well and truly fired. Just as keen photographers collect lenses and avid anglers have an array of rods, enthusiastic cooks will inevitably build up stocks of attractive serving dishes and plates, unusually shaped biscuit cutters and cake tins (which take up huge amounts of storage space!) and may well find themselves trying to find room in the store-cupboard for four different kinds of vinegar!

STORE-CUPBOARD BASICS

As well as simple equipment, you will also need some basic store-cupboard ingredients so that you do not have to buy everything from scratch every time you cook. Pages 21–52 look at the range of ingredients that will be useful, plus a number of products that make helpful standbys when you are called upon to whip up unexpected meals. A can of chopped tomatoes and a packet of dried pasta takes you well on the way to a decent meal. I would not suggest that you rush out and buy all the ingredients suggested in this chapter. Start with the essentials and, as you try new recipes, buy the ingredients required – your store-cupboard will soon expand. There is also advice about fresh produce and how to choose and prepare fruit, vegetables and meat.

STORING FOOD

It seems ironic that in an age when we know more than ever before about food hygiene and safety, and storage facilities in the kitchen are well advanced, food poisoning cases seem so frequent. Here a little learning is not a dangerous thing. Combined with a little common sense, it can help you to ensure that your food is stored in the safest possible way.

WHAT KIND OF KITCHEN?

Anybody who has even the slightest interest in cooking (or just in interior decoration) has a vision of a dream kitchen. Perhaps it is a rustic farmhouse kitchen, full of stripped-pine dressers and terracotta tiled floors. Maybe it is a gleaming picture of white units and lots of stainless steel. Whatever it is, it is quite unlikely to resemble the kitchen that most of us find ourselves using when we begin to cook. Pages 59–64 consider how to make best use of the facilities you have and how to plan a kitchen, should you be

7

given the opportunity. Kitchen safety, not always uppermost in the professional kitchen designer's mind, will also be covered. This is also the time to touch upon minor kitchen disasters that will occasionally befall even the most competent cook, and how they can best be remedied. Yes, most of them really can!

COOKING FOR FUN AND HEALTH

Cooking should be enjoyed. Enjoying your cooking means feeling confident in what you are doing, and pages 65–72 will explain exactly how to follow the recipes and start to solve some of the mysteries of cooking and cookery books.

Towards the end of this book, you will find some suggestions for entertaining. If you are just beginning your cookery career, it may seem a daunting task to feed yourself, never mind other people. Don't worry! You will be amazed at how quickly you master recipes and particular favourites will become your specialities. And remember, a simple, well cooked meal will be far better appreciated than an elaborate failure. People like to be fed – it saves them having to cook for themselves – so don't be shy about accepting offers of help with the washing up afterwards!

WHAT YOU
WILL NEED

The array of kitchen equipment is bewildering. After all, there are large stores that sell nothing but pans, bowls, tins and gadgets. Some of them are undeniably essential. Others are less so, but certainly make life easier, and some are just for those who have kitchen cupboards to fill. For example, a tin-opener is essential, a potato-masher is useful, but a fork and a bit more effort will produce an equally good result. On the other hand, a microwave crisp-maker does not appear in my list of suggested equipment!

In fact, you need only very basic equipment to make any of the recipes in this book. On the following pages, I will run through the things I consider essential, and will end with a checklist, so you can be sure you have all that you require. If this list looks a little daunting, you may not need it all at once. However, be sure to study any recipe you intend to make, to ensure that you have the equipment you need. By buying a new tool for your kitchen occasionally, you will be surprised how quickly you build up a useful range of gadgets. Bear in mind that others may "share" these. There is something to be said for buying cheap and cheerful versions instead of spending a lot on high quality ones that may get spoilt, or you may discover you hardly ever use.

PANS

The minimum you need is two saucepans. The first should be a small pan, preferably with a non-stick lining and a lid. This can be used for boiling milk, making sauces, scrambling eggs and cooking small amounts of vegetables. If you've ever tried to wash an ordinary pan after making porridge or scrambled eggs, you'll know why I suggest non-stick!

The second pan should be larger and also have a lid. It is possible to buy a pan with two small handles so that it can be used either on the hob (the top of the cooker) or in the oven, and this can double as a casserole dish. Quite a lot of recipes start by using the hob and finish their cooking in the oven, so such a pan can also save on washing up. There are cheap, enamelled pans available that are ideal, and they survive just about anything, except being dropped from a great height on to a concrete floor. Your frying pan should also be non-stick, and here I would seriously advise buying the cheapest you can find. Even if you have to replace it every couple of years, it is still more economical than investing in a really expensive one, which usually also has the disadvantage of being extremely heavy – and that's when it's empty!

BAKING TINS

A Swiss roll tin is the most versatile you can buy. You can use it for roasting, line it with pastry to make flans or use it to bake a sponge, which you can then halve to make a sandwich cake. A tin about 30 x 20cm (12 x 8 inches) and about 2cm ($^3/_4$ inch) deep is ideal. If you discover that baking is for you, then your baking tin collection will grow. A 12-hole bun tin and some 20cm (8 inch) round sandwich tins will be of immediate use and others will follow. My word of warning would be to remember storage space. Baking tins are not the most compressible of cooking items!

If you plan to make meatloaves, bread and tea cakes, you could consider buying a loaf tin, but this again is not essential.

CASSEROLES

If you manage to find a saucepan that doubles as a casserole, you may not need another casserole dish, but I have found that a medium-sized glass casserole with a lid is most useful. You can use it as a round cake tin; a glass dish is useful for making layered desserts; and the lid, turned upside down, doubles as a flan dish. So, if it's a casserole dish, a serving board, a baking tin and a flan dish, it probably earns its keep!

BOWLS

You really do need an assortment of bowls. At the very least, you need a large mixing bowl, about 3 litres (5 pints) in capacity and a small bowl, about 570ml (1 pint) in capacity, but you will probably find it useful to buy a set, which slot inside each other like Russian dolls and often have the bonus of clip-on lids. They make useful storage containers for fridge and freezer and can be used as airtight containers for biscuits and cakes.

CHOPPING BOARDS

Now that a good deal is known about food safety, it is advisable to have a minimum of two chopping boards – one for raw and one for cooked foods. Ideally, these should be made of a toughened plastic material and discarded if they become deeply scored. The danger is that bacteria can get into the grooves and resist your efforts to remove it by washing or wiping. This having been said, it is possible to use one chopping board, keeping one side for cooked food and the other for raw. This is not ideal, however, and you do need to remember which is which. However, there are very good household cleaners now available that contain anti-bacterial agents, and a good squirt of these after every use of your board should help.

KITCHEN SCALES

My mother-in-law rarely weighs anything, preferring to measure by eye, but most of us are less confident and prefer a little help. There are many different kinds of kitchen scales available in a large range of prices. Before you plump for the cheapest, check that it is reasonably strong, easily adjustable and that the bowl is of an adequate size. Quite often, you'll find scales that will weigh up to 2kg (4.4lbs) but only have a bowl large enough to hold half this amount. They may be a wee bit more expensive, but I prefer scales that have a large bowl sitting on a circular dial. You can add an ingredient, then turn the dial back to zero and add another. You have also gained an extra mixing bowl! I know that some people prefer to use the old-fashioned balance scales with weights. Personally I find them hard work, but this is really a matter of taste, although the fact that they are quite bulky and extremely heavy is worth remembering.

MEASURING JUGS AND SPOONS

These have to be considered as essential, especially in these days when milk comes in cartons, not bottles, so it is impossible to guess at the amount used. For light Yorkshire puddings and perfect custard, you need quite accurate measurements. A glass or clear plastic jug is the best to use, as the scale is easily read.

Measuring spoons are also useful, particularly as the amounts used of some spices in recipes are quite critical. Guessing a teaspoon of chilli powder could have dire consequences. As an economy, you could use an ordinary tablespoon and teaspoon, and as long as you always use the same ones, you can adjust your recipes as necessary. I would say that, on the whole, modern spoons tend to be quite shallow and hold less than measuring spoons.

WOODEN SPOONS

You will need a couple of wooden spoons and you may find these come in a set with a wooden spatula, which is a useful tool in your non-stick frying pan. I try to keep one wooden spoon for beating cakes and another for stirring chillies and curries, as strong flavours can permeate the wood.

KNIVES

Knives are important and you should have at least two. A 20cm (8 inch) cook's knife, with a triangular, straight blade, tapering to a point, is essential for chopping such ingredients as herbs, nuts and onions. A small, flexible, vegetable knife is necessary for peeling and more intricate work. At this point, a vegetable-peeler is an optional extra, but it is probably worth investing in a cheap one if you plan to peel many carrots or parsnips.

OTHER UTENSILS

Tin-openers

As previously mentioned, a tin-opener is essential. More expensive models are now available that do not leave any jagged or sharp edges. You may prefer to pay less, but you will need to be more careful!

Spatulas and pastry brushes

When baking, two pieces of equipment you should not be without are a flexible plastic spatula, for scraping out bowls, and a pastry brush, both for oiling cake tins and for glazing the tops of scones and pies.

Slotted spoons

A slotted spoon is useful for lifting boiled eggs out of their cooking water and straining small amounts of vegetables.

Palette knives and fish slices

A palette knife or fish slice is essential for removing biscuits from baking tray to cooling rack and fried eggs from pan to plate. I favour the palette knife, which, with its narrower blade, I find more versatile and flexible, but really it is a matter of personal preference. If you can afford both, so much the better.

Whisks and mashers

A wire whisk and a potato-masher are useful to have but can be replaced by a fork and some elbow grease. Storage space and how much you like mashed potatoes will have a part to play here!

Garlic-crushers

A garlic-crusher is useful but is not absolutely essential. You can either chop your garlic finely or try sprinkling a little salt on a chopping board (to give some friction), laying on the peeled clove of garlic and covering it with the side of a knife. Then thump this with the end of your fist and the garlic will crush.

Lemon-squeezers

Here is another gadget that really only has one use but takes up space. If you cut a lemon in half, jab the prongs of a fork into the cut edge and squeeze, while twisting the fork, you can get a lot of juice out of the fruit.

Sieves

You will definitely need a sieve. If you buy a reasonably large one, you can also use it as a colander to strain vegetables, but make sure it is thoroughly dry before you next try to sieve flour. Your sieve will also be necessary for puréeing fruit and soups. For this reason, I would suggest a metal mesh, as it is more robust.

Rolling pins

If you intend to make lots of pastries and biscuits, you will want to invest in a rolling pin. It is also useful for crushing biscuits and doubles as a steak hammer for tenderising meat. A wooden rolling pin is fine. I prefer the type that is just a straight cylinder and has no handles. If you are rolling a large sheet of pastry, the handles can sometimes mark the dough at the edges. A wine bottle makes a reasonable substitute, though I wouldn't suggest you use one to hammer steaks!

Cheese-graters

A cheese-grater is a must, not just for the obvious, but also for grating the zest from oranges and lemons, grating chocolate and making breadcrumbs. Choose a grater that has a range of holes. The large flat ones are ideal for cheese; the big spiky ones make perfect breadcrumbs, while the small spiky ones zest citrus fruit.

Cooling racks

If you plan to do a lot of baking, you will need a cooling rack or two. You can use the rack out of the grill, but often the spaces between the bars are quite large and biscuits can fall through. I would choose racks that have a small, square grid.

LARGER ITEMS

Kettles

This should probably come before any other piece of equipment, because a sustaining mug of coffee or comforting cup of tea is sometimes all that will do. Obviously, you can have a whistling kettle on the hob, but most people plump for an electric one, preferably with an automatic cut-off switch. If you are on your own, it is worth considering the jug-type kettle, where less water is required to cover the element and you can literally boil a mug full. Of course, in theory you could save the cost of a kettle by boiling water in a pan on the hob, but somehow it just doesn't taste the same!

Food processors and food mixers

Once someone has owned a food processor, they usually wonder how they ever managed without one. However, they are fairly bulky to store and there are quite a few bits and pieces when it comes to washing up, although by chopping and mixing in the right order, you can usually avoid having to wash up between operations.

A hand-held mixer is also a very handy piece of equipment. It is just two little whisks in a handle, with a choice of three speeds. It is marvellous for cake-making, egg-whisking, cream-whipping and so on. If a recipe calls for whisked egg whites and beaten cream, you can dive into the egg-white bowl and then, without any need for washing up, move on to the cream. Neither food processors nor mixers are essential – after all, our great-grandmothers managed perfectly well without them – but they will make light work of many of the recipes in this book.

Microwave ovens

If you are under 25, you probably consider this to be as indispens-able as a computer. I wouldn't be without one, not to heat up ready-meals or cook Sunday lunch, as some seem able to do, but as an extremely useful tool. Microwave ovens make excellent scrambled eggs, melt chocolate, dissolve jellies and soften butter in seconds. They make wonderful custard and white sauces and, of course, are splendid for defrosting, when you remember half an hour before supper that you failed to remove the pork chops from the freezer that morning!

If you decide to buy a microwave, consider carefully what you will use it for. If, like me, you think you will use it more as a handy gadget than an oven, then buy the smallest, cheapest one you can find. Power ratings and dozens of settings are of no real interest. If you want to use it to cook full meals, then look for a combination one, which incorporates a grill and can brown and crisp food, two talents that traditional microwaves certainly lack. Remember, you may have to buy equipment specifically for the microwave: most metal containers cannot be used in them and not all plastics are microwave-proof.

I have not given microwave instructions in this book as not everybody will have access to one, but if you study the handbook supplied with the oven, you will soon be able to adapt various recipes to use it. For example, biscuits (such as flapjacks) and cakes (such as gingerbread), which are made by melting and mixing, can be cooked in the microwave, and by using the same bowl to melt the fat and syrup that you use to make the mix, you can also save on washing up. Remember to select a big enough bowl at the outset, even if the butter does look a bit lost in it initially.

Toaster

A toaster is only a necessity if you don't have a grill. If you are preparing toast for several people, the grill is probably the quickest option anyway, but, of course, you do have to keep your eye on it, because it is a known fact that toast will only burn if you turn your back on it! There are now toasters available that are wide enough to take crumpets and teacakes, which is quite an advantage.

EQUIPMENT CHECKLIST

The following is the list of kitchen equipment you will need to tackle the recipes in this book. Those marked with an asterisk (*) are not absolutely essential and alternatives have been discussed in the previous pages. Please note that capacity suggestions are approximate. If you find a slightly smaller or larger item that you like, it should be fine.

Saucepans: one small, non-stick with lid, 570ml (1 pint) capacity
            one larger with lid, 2 litre (3 pint) capacity
Frying pan: preferably non-stick
Glass casserole dish with lid: 3 litre (5 pint) capacity
Large mixing bowl: 3 litre (5 pint) capacity
Small mixing bowl: 570ml (1 pint) capacity
Swiss roll tin: 30 x 20 x 2cm (12 x 8 x 3/4 inches)
*Loaf tin
*Cooling rack
Wooden spoons: at least 2 of different sizes
*Wooden spatula
*Slotted spoon

Palette knife or fish slice
Flexible plastic spatula
Pastry brush
Tin-opener
*Garlic-crusher
Small vegetable knife
Cook's knife: 20cm (8 inch) blade
*Vegetable-peeler
Chopping boards: at least 2, for raw and cooked food
Cheese-grater
Measuring jug
Measuring spoons
*Lemon-squeezer
*Rolling pin
*Apple-corer
Kitchen scales
Large sieve: ideally with metal mesh
*Wire whisk
*Potato-masher
Kettle
*Microwave oven
*Food processor
*Food mixer
*Toaster

I am assuming that you have a collection of plates, mugs, dishes and glasses. Relatives and friends seem only too happy to unearth cast-offs from the attic when they know you are setting up on your own (and remember, it's now considered quite trendy if these don't match). Knives, forks, teaspoons and serving spoons will probably also come your way. If you do need to invest, mail-order catalogues often have very good deals that provide crockery, cutlery, glass and sometimes table-mats and tea-towels as well.

BUYING
THE BASICS

Your shopping strategy will depend on three things: your storage space, how easy it is to fit shopping into your weekly schedule, and how organised you are! If you are sharing a fridge and have a small amount of cupboard space to hold your supplies, shopping in bulk once a month is not really for you. On the other hand, if the nearest food shop is three bus rides and a two-mile walk away, you will not want to have to pop out every time you run out of tea bags.

Some people like to plan a week's or even a fortnight's menus in advance and can then shop specifically for the items they need. Others prefer to throw open the cupboard doors and see what appeals for supper that evening. A combination of these two approaches is probably the ideal route. It is best to shop at least weekly for fresh meat, fruit, vegetables and dairy produce. As these are perishable and quite expensive, you will need to have some idea of when you will eat them. This doesn't mean that you have to have a rigid routine of mince on Wednesday, chops on Thursday and fish on Friday, but you should at least aim to have the makings of three main meals with appropriate vegetables.

Alongside your fresh produce, it will also be helpful to have some store-cupboard meal options. A packet of pasta, a tin of chopped tomatoes and a tin of tuna will always produce a meal. A range of canned goods is a useful standby. I would suggest sweetcorn, red kidney beans, baked beans, mince in gravy, corned beef and evaporated milk as handy store-cupboard basics that will ensure you never go hungry.

While it is possible to give a definitive list of the equipment you will need to make any of the recipes in this book, it is not so simple to give a list of all the ingredients required. Nor would it be possible for you to stock up on everything beforehand, for, of course, there will be fresh produce to be included. However, I can suggest a range of products that you should always have to hand. From this basic stock, you will find yourself buying one or two ingredients each time you try out a new recipe. In that way, you will gradually build up your store-cupboard. Many of the ingredients, such as golden syrup, baking powder and porridge oats, are not those that you will use every day, but they have a long shelf life when stored in appropriate conditions. If you decide to make a German apple cake, for example, you may have to buy apples, ground cinnamon and walnuts, in addition to your available stores. Later, when you decide to make baked apples, you will find that it is only the apples you need to buy, – you already have the rest of the ingredients in your store-cupboard.

You will find that basic ingredients come in a number of sizes. Flour, for example, may be bought in 500g or 1.5kg packs. You will need to decide which is the better buy. The larger pack will almost certainly be cheaper, gram for gram, but will you use it up quickly enough and do you have room to store it? You will quickly find out which are the ingredients that you use regularly, and are therefore worth buying in large amounts, and which you only need occasionally, in small packets. The same choice faces you if a supermarket offers savings when you buy two packets of the same product instead of one, or has a "buy two, get one free" promotion. If you have enough storage space and the items have a long shelf life, such as canned goods, washing-up liquid or dry packet foods, then it may well be worthwhile, although this depends on the flexibility of your weekly budget.

When shopping for any product, it is worth looking out for a store's own-label goods. These are usually considerably cheaper than the recognised brands, but still of excellent quality. Try a small packet or can first to check that you like the product, before bulk buying.

It is worth considering some essential store-cupboard items in more detail.

FLOUR

Once there was simply a choice between plain and self-raising flour. The latter includes raising agents, such as baking powder, so that you don't have to add them. You could also just buy plain flour and sift in these raising agents yourself as necessary, but it is easier to have a bag of each in your store-cupboard. Plain flour is used for making most pastries and biscuits, while self-raising flour is used in cakes and sponges – anything where you need a light texture.

It is possible to buy wholemeal flour in both plain and self-raising varieties. As the name suggests, this is made from the whole grain of the wheat and so is richer in fibre than white flour.

Also available is something called strong plain flour, used in breadmaking and other yeast cookery, and superfine flours for delicate baked goods. These more specialist flours are much more expensive. Unless you are making something extra special, I would suggest that you buy the cheapest basic flours you can find, remembering always to sift them before you use them.

Cornflour is essential. It is not normally used for baking, but for thickening soups, sauces and casseroles. It is worth tipping the cornflour into a clean, dry jam jar, as you will probably use it frequently and the packet will get crumpled and messy. Do label the jam jar!

SUGARS AND SYRUPS

These products, too, are available in an enormous variety of forms, from the finest white sugar to dark and sticky muscovado. If you only have storage space for one kind, I would suggest that you buy caster sugar, which is finer than ordinary granulated. It is a little more expensive but ideal for cakes and baking, and will taste no different if you stir it into your tea!

Icing sugar has been very finely powdered and, as well as being used for icings and frostings, is useful in fruit purées and milk drinks because it dissolves quickly and easily.

Demerara sugar is golden brown and has quite large crystals. For this reason, it is ideal when you want to retain a crunchy, sugary texture, such as in a crumble mix or topping.

Soft brown sugars are wonderfully moist and can be either light or dark in colour. The richest and darkest is muscovado, which has a molasses-like flavour and is used in rich fruit cakes and Christmas puddings. For general-purpose baking, a light, soft brown sugar is a good all-rounder for moist or sticky dishes, such as gingerbread and baked bananas.

You may also come across cubed (both white and brown) sugar, coffee crystals and golden granulated sugar. For special occasions, you may want to offer cubes or crystals to guests, but, unless you entertain very regularly, you are likely to find half-used packets of these in the back of your cupboard months later.

For those of us with a sweet tooth, a tin of golden syrup is a store-cupboard essential, because there are days when only a syrup pudding will do! Syrup and treacle are often confused, for when we talk of treacle pudding and treacle tart, we usually expect them to be made of golden syrup. Real treacle is rich and black. It is an essential ingredient in most gingerbread and some very rich fruit cakes, but it has a distinctive taste and should be used quite sparingly. It can often be replaced, in part or completely, by golden syrup.

RICE AND PASTA

Twenty years ago, cooking a meal that included rice or pasta was considered rather daring (except for rice pudding and macaroni cheese, of course). Now that we have adopted so many dishes from other countries as favourite recipes, rice and pasta form a major part of most people's diets and provide a useful source of carbohydrate for energy.

Once again, the choice is immense. For savoury cooking, you need a long grain rice. I would suggest that you buy one labelled "easy cook". You could choose white or brown rice. Brown usually takes a little longer to cook than white, which is not always convenient, but it does contain fibre and has a delicious, nutty taste and texture.

Basmati rice is specifically for Indian cookery and you will sometimes find it sold mixed with wild rice, which, just to complicate matters, is not rice at all, but actually a grass seed. For a true risotto, you should use arborio rice, which has short, fat grains and looks quite similar to our traditional pudding rice.

If you think that the choice of rices is vast, it is nothing compared to the selection of pastas. As we are considering store-cupboard buys here, I will concentrate on dried pasta, but look in the chilled cabinet of your supermarket occasionally and treat yourself to some fresh pasta, delicious with just a sprinkling of freshly ground black pepper and a dash of olive oil. Meanwhile, back at the dried pasta counter, you are likely to be bewildered by the choice of shapes and colours. The colours are achieved by the inclusion of spinach, beetroot, tomato purée and so on in the pasta dough. These additions do not add very much flavour but look attractive.

Different pasta shapes all have special Italian names: tagliatelle, spaghetti, rigatoni, penne, fusilli, conchiglie ... the list goes on and on. Basically, they all *taste* the same, but they have different uses. If you are serving a fairly runny sauce over pasta, then the shell-shaped pieces will help to catch it. A thick sauce is better over ribbon pasta or spaghetti. Tiny pasta shapes, designed to go in soups and stews, are also available. The message here is to experiment – luckily pasta is a relatively cheap ingredient – and find the type you like best.

STOCK CUBES

It is worth having chicken, beef and vegetable stock cubes to hand. Buy a decent quality cube because you are adding stock to give flavour, and coloured water will not achieve this. Stock is the basis of many dishes. Of course, you *can* make your own by boiling bones for hours, but a quickly crumbled cube and a jug of boiling water will work just as well for most occasions. If you do feel the need for something a little more special, look in the chilled cabinet of your food store, where it is now often possible to buy tubs of ready-made stock.

CANNED VEGETABLES AND FRUIT

My store-cupboard always contains tins of sweetcorn, red kidney beans, chopped tomatoes and baked beans. A tin of pineapple chunks in natural juice is also tucked away for emergencies! Sweetcorn can be used to add colour and flavour to many dishes, and can also help to stretch them a little further. Casseroles, chillies, soups, omelettes, rice dishes and pasta can all have the sweetcorn treatment. In these days of healthy eating, you may prefer to use the canned sweetcorn with no added sugar or salt, although I find this rather horrid. I'm not a huge fan of the tins that contain pieces of red and green pepper either – their flavour seems to dominate everything else. Of course, all this is simply a question of personal taste.

Red kidney beans also have a great ability to extend dishes. You will find that a lot of sediment gathers at the bottom of the can. You can empty the beans into a sieve and drain them in cold water, but to save washing up, I undo the tin, not entirely removing the lid, press the lid down and drain out the liquid. I then fill up the can (still containing the beans) with cold water and slosh it about before draining again. If you do this a couple of

times, you will get rid of all the sludge. It is actually much quicker and simpler to do than to describe!

Tinned tomatoes would also be on my must-have list. With a squeeze of tomato purée and a grind of black pepper, you have an instant pasta sauce. I tend to buy the chopped tomatoes in natural juice, although the whole ones are much cheaper, and if you open the can at one end and run a sharp knife through them a few times, you soon have chopped tomatoes. It is possible to buy canned tomatoes with added herbs, onion, garlic or olive oil. These are a reasonable buy if speed is of the essence, but you will get a better flavour if you add these ingredients yourself.

It almost goes without saying that baked beans are a store-cupboard essential. They are, after all, the ultimate snack, and you will find them included in several of the recipes in this book. Here I become more virtuous – I actually prefer the varieties with reduced sugar and salt – but again, you may feel differently. People tend to be very loyal to their own brand of baked beans and can always tell if you try to slip in a cheap substitute. (In my experience, this is true of tomato ketchup, as well.)

Tinned fruit has come a long way from the fruit cocktail in syrup that used to be dished up for Sunday tea (with tinned cream, of course). Fruits in natural juices have an excellent flavour and make good purées. A tin of apricot halves is a useful standby and forms the basis of a number of desserts.

CANNED MEAT AND FISH

A tin of tuna in brine, a small can of corned beef and a tin of salmon would be my recommendations. If you have these, you have the makings of tuna fish pie (page 174), corned beef hash (page 144) and fishcakes, salmon sandwiches or any number of other dishes. Canned meat and fish have an incredibly long (though not indefinite) shelf life and are ideal store-cupboard ingredients. If you like them, tinned frankfurters, mince in gravy and chicken in white sauce are also useful standbys.

HERBS AND SPICES

This is an enormous subject area that could easily fill a book by itself. If you are a curry enthusiast, you will have a cupboard full of ground cumin, cardamom pods and garam masala, but for the less specialist cook, there are a number of dried herbs and spices that are worth keeping in stock.

Obviously, you will need salt and pepper. Finely ground sea salt would be my choice, and I would also suggest that you treat yourself to a pepper mill. A cheap plastic one is fine. Freshly ground black pepper gives a boost to everything from mashed potatoes to poached salmon. Buy whole black peppercorns for grinding. It is probably worthwhile having a shaker of ready-ground white pepper as well.

I'd suggest that you invest in a medium-strength chilli powder. Most of the time, it is pointless being macho and buying a really hot one – just use more of the slightly milder one and you will be adding flavour as well as heat. A good quality curry paste should be fine for basic curry making. You can start buying and grinding your own whole spices if you become really enthusiastic.

Ground cinnamon, ground ginger and ground mixed spice should cover most of your baking needs, although you may like to keep a sachet of whole cloves if you are an apple-pie fan, and ground nutmeg if you like the skin on rice puddings.

Dried herbs do not have the flavour or colour of freshly chopped ones, but parsley, thyme, sage and bay leaves are all robust enough to survive the drying process. Modern freeze-drying techniques also ensure that the leaves keep their colour quite well.

I shall include mustard powder in this section, as I find that I use it in many recipes. Mustard has the ability to bring out cheese flavours, so add a pinch to a cheese sauce or to a cheese straw recipe. Mustard also has emulsifying properties. This means that it helps oils to mix with liquids instead of separating out. It is therefore a very useful ingredient when making oil and vinegar dressings or mayonnaise.

OILS AND FATS

In recent years there has been a good deal of advice on which oils are best for our health, alongside warnings that too much fat and oil is bad for us in general. Health advice does seem to change fairly frequently, as new discoveries and studies are made, but at the moment, my advice would be as follows.

For a general-purpose oil, choose one that is labelled "high in polyunsaturates". Sunflower oil is good and economical.

It is also worthwhile treating yourself to a bottle of olive oil – virgin, cold-pressed is considered to be the best. This is delicious in salad dressings and trickled over pasta. It also forms a large part of the Mediterranean diet, which experts currently hold to be a healthy one to follow.

There are a number of more exotic oils, such as sesame oil (wonderful in stir-fries), groundnut oil, walnut oil, grapeseed oil and so on. Nut oils make wonderful salad dressings but they are very expensive for everyday use.

As with oils, fats are a minefield of nutritional claims and counter-claims. Margarines may have a higher proportion of the healthier polyunsaturated fats than butter, but they are also highly processed from a wide variety of ingredients. Butter usually only has one added ingredient: salt. Whatever you choose, use it in moderation.

To my absolute amazement, the other day I spotted a packet of suet labelled as "25% reduced fat". Purely in the interests of research (of course!), I used it to make a jam rolypoly and I can report that it was most successful. Of course, it is still 75% fat, so one could not advocate its daily use, but every little helps.

When it comes to baking, your choices are really butter, hard or block margarine, and soft margarine. Where a real buttery flavour is essential, such as in shortbread, use real butter, but for most cakes, soft margarine is fine. As the name suggests, it does not emerge rock hard from the fridge and is therefore easier to mix with other ingredients. At a push, it can be used for most things, although traditionalists would say that you should use hard fat when making pastry or other dishes that use the "rubbing-in" method. In fact, you can usually use soft margarine, which rubs in much more easily, and simply chill the dough in the fridge before you use it (if you don't, it will be softer than usual and difficult to roll out and handle). Better still, you can buy ready-made pastry and save a lot of time and mess. This is definitely worth doing with puff and flaky pastry, and the results are very good.

JAMS AND SPREADS

If you only have room in your store-cupboard for one jam, it should probably be apricot. This can be used to fill cakes, bind ingredients together and glaze cakes and desserts. But it would be a pity to exclude for ever some of the other delicious flavours available: strawberry jam with scones and cream, damson jam oozing out of a jam rolypoly, cherry jam spread thickly on warm, flaky croissants. Of course, the choice is yours.

You may also feel that you need some marmalade for your toast, but when it comes to toast-toppings, the choice is enormous. Peanut butter, chocolate spread (with or without nuts), white chocolate spread, toffee spread, marshmallow spread (yes, really!), honey in any number of flavours (and set or runny, of course), and yeast extract spread, which you've probably been eating since you first had teeth, are all readily available. I'm a great believer in the therapeutic powers of a thick slice of warm toast, oozing with butter (this is no time for low-calorie substitutes) and a thick layer of jam or spread.

BAKING INGREDIENTS

You may not be particularly interested in baking, but if you are, there are a number of quite specialist ingredients that you will need. Scones and Scotch pancakes need cream of tartar and bicarbonate of soda to make them light and well risen. You can buy these in small tubs that last for ages. A small bottle of vanilla essence will be essential – or you may prefer the more natural flavour of vanilla extract, although this *is* more expensive. Perhaps you would like to have some food colours and some sprinkle-on decorations, such as hundreds and thousands or chocolate vermicelli. Be warned, hovering too long in the baking section of your food store can cause serious damage to your wallet and waistline!

DRIED FRUIT AND NUTS

Usually found next to the baking section, dried fruit used to consist only of sultanas, currants and raisins. You will now find dried cherries, mangoes and cranberries, as well as bananas and pineapples. It's a good idea to keep a packet of dried apricots handy, although they may never reach a recipe as the "no-need-to-soak" variety make a delicious snack straight from the packet. If you require more traditional dried fruit for a cake or pudding, it is possible to buy a pack of mixed sultanas, currants, raisins and mixed peel, which saves on storage space. A tub of glacé cherries is a useful standby for baking and decoration. You can now buy these with natural (rather than chemical) colouring.

Suppliers have taken all the hard work out of baking with pre-packed nuts. Almonds, for example, always used to be available only with the brown skin on. They needed blanching, by covering them with boiling water and popping them out of their skins, before chopping. Now, you can buy them blanched, flaked, chopped, toasted and ground. Of course, you pay for the privilege, so you will need to balance convenience against cost. Walnuts are available as halves or pieces. The latter are quite a bit cheaper and as, nine times out of ten, you are going to chop them up anyway, they make a worthwhile saving. Flaked almonds and walnut pieces are useful to have in the store-cupboard. If you like coconut, add a bag of desiccated (dried) coconut too.

HOT AND COLD DRINKS

Even if you do not drink tea or coffee yourself, you may need to have them to offer to visitors. For everyday drinking, instant coffee is acceptable, although I feel that it is worth buying a decent brand. Personally, I would rather drink half the quantity of a good coffee than double the amount of some of the cheaper options. For special occasions, you might like to consider buying a cafetiere, which works by plunging hot water through ground coffee. You will need to buy ground coffee labelled as suitable for cafetieres, as that labelled for filters is ground much more finely and would jam up the plunger! With all coffees nowadays, you have the choice of decaffeinated varieties.

There is now a vast range of teas available, bagged or loose, and fruit and herb teas are becoming increasingly popular as healthy alternatives. If you live in a bedsit or flat, getting rid of tea leaves can be a nightmare – you may well find tea bags much more convenient. This need not prevent you from trying some choice teas: Darjeeling, Earl Grey and camomile are all available in this form.

After a long walk in winter, there is nothing nicer than wrapping yourself round a mug of hot chocolate. You can make this by adding cocoa powder or drinking chocolate powder to hot milk, or use one of the instant mixes available, to which you simply add boiling water. There is an astonishing range of flavours of these: plain, white and milk chocolate, with orange, mint, banana, coffee and toffee, to name just a few. I always keep cocoa powder in the house as well, but to use for cooking, not drinking. It is essential that you use cocoa when a recipe asks for it – neither drinking chocolate nor instant varieties have the flavour or consistency you need.

Fruit juice can be bought in cartons that will keep it fresh without chilling as long as they remain unopened. This helps to save on valuable fridge space. As well as the more common orange, pineapple, grapefruit and apple juices, you can now buy exotic juice blends to ring the changes. Simpler mixtures of cranberry and apple, or orange and raspberry, are also delicious.

Many people now prefer to use bottled water for drinking. Indeed, tap waters do seem to vary in flavour. In addition to the choice of plain or carbonated, there are also flavoured waters, containing fruit extracts.

Carbonated drinks used to be full of sugar and not considered very nutritionally sound. Modern alternatives include virtually sugar-free drinks – perhaps a healthier option.

The whole area of alcoholic drinks is too vast to cover here, but from a cooking point of view, a half bottle of brandy and a bottle of sherry are useful. If a recipe calls for a small amount of a spirit or liqueur, you can always buy a miniature. If you need a little wine for a dish, it may be a mistake to buy too cheap a variety, as you will probably drink the remainder!

SUNDRY STORE-CUPBOARD ITEMS

Most of the items in this list are designed to add flavour, either as part of a dish or served alongside it.

Tomato purée

You can buy this in a can, jar or tube. I think that it keeps better in a tube. You can squirt out a little and keep the tube in the fridge. Once you open a can or jar, it has to be used fairly quickly. Tomato purée adds a richness and tomato flavour to stews and pasta sauces that is difficult to achieve with tinned tomatoes alone.

Sauces and vinegars

Worcestershire sauce can be used to pep up any number of dishes. Try a dash in cheese sauces, casseroles and stir-fries. Because it has a distinct flavour, you literally only need a few drops, so a bottle lasts a long time.

There are lots of flavoured vinegars on the market these days. You will probably need ordinary malt vinegar for those evenings when the kitchen loses its appeal and the pull of the chip shop wins. Buy a bottle that already has a sprinkler on the top to avoid drowning your chips! White and red wine vinegars add a delicious flavour to salad dressings, as does cider vinegar. Perhaps choose one of these first and then try another one when you run out. It's probably not a good idea to buy a bottle of red wine vinegar and think that it will do for everything – unless you like your chips pink! Balsamic vinegar has only recently become widely available here. It is absolutely delicious and ruinously expensive. A dash in casseroles and salad dressings certainly gives a wonderful flavour, but at a luxurious price.

Whether you consider brown sauce, tomato ketchup and salad cream as essentials is up to you. The latter is also available in lower-calorie varieties, as is mayonnaise.

Mashed potato

Nothing beats creamy mashed potato with some dishes, but if you are serving it as a vegetable, do not be tempted to offer the instant variety. Experience has taught me that even if you beat in an awful lot of butter and black pepper, the unmistakable flavour is still there in the background. However, you may find it acceptable in fish cakes, or, at a push, on top of a cottage pie, but do buy a quality brand.

Breakfast cereals and biscuits

A packet of your favourite breakfast cereal is a useful standby, not just for breakfast but as a reasonably nutritious snack at any time of the day.

It is also useful to have a packet of cream crackers or other plain biscuits handy. If you have a lump of cheese in the fridge, you will always have a savoury snack or the means of adding an extra course to a meal.

Personally, I also consider a packet of digestive biscuits essential, but I do know people who wouldn't dream of wandering down the biscuit aisle of their food store. Again, it's your choice.

MILK AND MILK PRODUCTS

You can buy fresh or UHT milk. The latter has been heated to a high enough temperature to kill off any nasty bugs and is then packaged so that it can be stored for several months and doesn't need to be refrigerated until opened. The disadvantage is that this process does something to the flavour of the milk, which you may well dislike. However, while this is true of full-fat and semi-skimmed milks, skimmed milk survives the process quite well. It is much more difficult to detect whether skimmed milk is fresh or UHT. If you are not regularly at home or cannot get to the shops easily, that is worth considering. There is also the plus point that skimmed milk is a healthier option (except for very young children). At the very least, a couple of cartons of UHT skimmed milk in the cupboard is probably a sound idea.

You may like to keep a can of condensed milk handy for a possible banoffee pie (see page 191) or wicked coffee slice (page 212), or you may prefer to keep temptation at bay. A tin or carton of ready-made custard means that you can quickly make a fruit fool in an emergency. I also like to keep a tin of rice pudding in the house. Layered with tinned apricots in natural juice, it makes a quick but delicious dessert, and served hot with a dollop of jam or golden syrup, it is instant comfort food.

IN THE REFRIGERATOR

This category includes products that have to be bought very fresh, such as meat, fish, dairy products and salad vegetables, but there are also a number of items that will lurk happily in your fridge for several weeks.

Cheese

A piece of well-flavoured cheddar is essential. You will find that most cheese is now labelled as suitable for vegetarians, but it is worth checking the label if this is important to you. A small piece of parmesan cheese will add a finishing touch when grated on to pasta dishes, or you can buy it in drums, ready grated. This doesn't have quite such a good flavour, but it is better than nothing.

Eggs

Keep half a dozen eggs in the fridge. You will always be able to make a quick omelette. Many people now feel that it is kindest to try to buy free-range eggs where possible, but do check the box carefully, as wording and pictures can be a bit misleading about the lives of the egg-producers. In fact, eggs should ideally be kept in a cool place but not in the fridge, but this is not always practical. If time allows, try to leave eggs at room temperature for a while before boiling them, as this will help to prevent the shells from cracking.

Condiments and flavourings

These days you are always likely to find your fridge full of little jars and bottles. This is because the recent push to remove as many additives as possible from foods has meant that items that could once be stored in the store-cupboard now bear the legend "refrigerate after opening", as the preservative has been removed. A squeezy bottle of lemon juice, a jar or mayonnaise and a tube of tomato purée will also need a space.

Bread

This is included here because it is a perishable item, but it is a mistake to keep it in the fridge. Chilled temperatures actually speed up the staling process, so bread is better kept, covered, in the kitchen.

VEGETABLES AND FRUIT

The vegetable recipe section of this book (from page 105) gives some tips on storage of individual vegetables. Most are best bought fresh, but a number do store quite successfully. Potatoes, swedes, turnips and parsnips will keep for several weeks if stored in cool, dark conditions. Always empty them out of any plastic bags as these cause the vegetables to sweat and go mouldy.

Onions and garlic will keep in the kitchen for several weeks. A head of garlic, which separates into perhaps eight cloves, will last for some time, since recipes usually only call for one or two cloves. I would suggest that you buy smallish onions. You can always use two if a recipe asks for a large onion, and it saves having to store a smelly half-onion in the fridge.

A number of vegetables, however, store quite well in the fridge. Carrots will keep for ages and celery, leeks and courgettes also last well. Make sure that the vegetables are in good condition when you buy them. A firm white or red cabbage will also keep well while it is whole but will deteriorate quite quickly once cut.

When buying fruit that you hope to keep, again choose sound specimens with no obvious blemishes, preferably slightly under-ripe. Keep them in a cool place, but not in the fridge. Apples, whether of the eating or cooking variety, keep well, as do most citrus fruits. Bananas, grapes and soft fruits do not store so well. They should be bought at the peak of perfection and eaten quickly. As with vegetables, it is important to remove fruits from plastic bags after buying, so that they are well ventilated.

MEAT AND FISH

Most meat and fish has a fairly limited life. The fresher you can buy it, the better. Modern packaging techniques can help to prolong storage time, particularly with cured meats such as ham and bacon. These are either packed under vacuum, when the plastic is sucked tight against the meat and there is no room for any air to cause spoilage, or they are packed in a special gas mixture that helps to preserve the meat. Remember that this will only extend the life of the meat once it remains unopened. Once the seal is broken, the meat must be eaten up quite quickly. This extended life means that it is worthwhile keeping a packet of bacon in the fridge. You can now buy much leaner varieties, some having reduced salt as well. There is also a product, actually made of cured turkey meat, that behaves and tastes like bacon but is virtually fat free.

Many of the main-course dishes in this book contain mince. This is available in a number of varieties. Beef mince is the most common: it may be coarsely or finely minced and the fat content can vary from about 5% to 25%. A 10–12% fat content is a good compromise between health and palatability, as the fat in meat helps give succulence and flavour. Pork, lamb and even venison mince is quite readily available, as is turkey mince, which again is a healthier option. Vegetarians can use the vegetable mince substitutes that are now found in most food stores. Although many recipes call for beef mince, it is worth experimenting with other kinds.

Chicken has become the nation's most popular meat and its attractions are obvious. It is low in fat and high in protein, giving it a healthy image. It is also very adaptable, having a mild flavour that complements many dishes. Modern farming methods also mean that it is relatively cheap. You may wish to buy free-range chickens as a kinder option, but if you buy your chicken from a reputable butcher or supermarket, the birds are likely to have been reared and processed humanely.

You will find quite a choice of cuts apart from the whole birds. Drumsticks, thighs and whole legs are ideal for casseroles, while breast portions are perfect for baked chicken parcels (see page 235) and boneless breast fillets are excellent cut into strips and used in stir-fries and other quick-cook recipes. Remember to remove the skin if you are counting calories, as this is where most of the fat hides.

When it comes to buying meat, the inexperienced cook can sometimes feel daunted in a butcher's shop. Although you may pay a little more for pre-packaged meat in a supermarket, it is often easier to see all the cuts displayed. It can also be simpler to judge how much you require when you see 225g (8oz) actually laid out in a packet. You will often find that the packaging includes serving suggestions on the label. This may range from a simple nudge in the right direction, such as "ideal for stews and casseroles", to a full-blown recipe. Pre-packaged meat will have a use-by date and suggested storage conditions on the label, and you can pop the packs straight into the fridge or freezer when you get home. Most pre-packaged meats will have a small absorbent pad in the base of the pack to catch any drips and juices. In a hurry, I have on occasion cooked this with the joint, and while it isn't harmful, it doesn't exactly add to the flavour either, so I would strongly recommend removing this!

Unless you really cannot bear to handle raw meat, don't pay extra for cubed stewing steak or sliced liver. You can easily do this yourself. What is more, it will be cut to the size *you* want and not what someone else dictates.

If you have access to a freezer, you will find that it is often more economical to buy larger packets of meat and, once home, split them into smaller amounts and freeze them. If you are catering for one or two, you can divide sausages up this way, and I can certainly say that if you freeze a whole packet of sausages, it is almost impossible to separate them without defrosting the whole lot. Breaking meat down into smaller amounts may help you to eat less as well, if that is an issue.

Always buy meat and fish that looks fresh and appetising. It should glisten and be a good colour. Any fat should be white. Bear in mind that a small amount of fat, marbled through the meat, will give it a much better flavour than most very lean meat. This fat will largely cook out, but it will add succulence to the meat. Nowadays, it seems that hardly a week goes by without a health scare about one meat or another. Obviously, you should listen to the reports, but be sensible and hear all sides. You can then make a reasoned judgement about how you should react. I am inclined to think that if you buy your meat from a reputable butcher or supermarket, you have little to fear, but the final decision is yours.

Fresh fish should be eaten within a day or two of purchase to ensure that it is at its best. Look carefully at labels because packaged fish has often been previously frozen and then thawed. This means that you should not freeze it again. High-street fishmongers are disappearing at an alarming rate. Not everyone lives near enough to the sea to buy freshly caught fish. However, many larger supermarkets now have fish counters, where trained staff should be able to advise you on the best cuts to buy, suitable storage and even recipe ideas. Considering that we are surrounded by sea, we eat remarkably little fish as a nation. This is a pity, as it is a versatile source of protein and tends to be lower in fat than many meats. If you live in a bedsit, you may want to invest in a can of air freshener along with your kippers – unfortunately a lingering smell is one result of fish cookery.

CONVENIENCE FOODS

The idea of this book is to encourage you to make your own meals, cheaper and tastier than buying them ready made. But, of course, there will be times when you are in a hurry or just too tired to cook. And there are some convenience foods that are well worth buying.

As mentioned above, I am a great advocate of buying ready-made pastry, whether chilled or frozen. I have a slight struggle with my conscience when a packet of shortcrust pastry (the kind usually used for flan cases) sneaks into my shopping trolley, because it is relatively straightforward to make, but no such qualms about puff or filo pastry. It takes forever to make and the finished results are rarely as good as the bought variety.

Some cook-in sauces are also a useful buy, and a bag of mixed, prepared salad can be more economical than buying lots of different lettuces and preparing them yourself.

Like every shopper, I feel that some products take convenience too far. Grated cheese would be an example for me. Grating cheese is neither a time-consuming nor a skilled task, so why pay someone to do it for you? I am also not very keen on the prepared vegetables that are now available. These include peeled and sliced carrots, prepared sprouts and even shredded cabbage. Apart from the fact that this at least doubles the cost of the vegetables, you are also losing valuable nutrients from the cut surfaces.

The secret with convenience foods is to decide whether the additional cost is worth it to you. As with many things, you are basically balancing time against money. If you are catering for one, then you probably have a stronger argument for buying ready-made dishes, since you will have no wastage. On the other hand, careful shopping and planning could avoid that anyway.

Perhaps one of the best ways to use convenience foods is to add your own personal touch to them. In the recipe for fish pie (page 173), I've used frozen cod in sauce to make a "home-made" dish. Or you could buy a basic cheese and tomato pizza and add your own choice of salami, tuna, prawn, peppers or whatever to give it a fresher quality.

Finally, if you are on a diet (and for some of us that's rather often), some of the fresh and frozen calorie-counted and low-fat meals are very good. They ensure that you have no left-overs to nibble and keep you safely out of the kitchen!

NON-FOOD ITEMS

All kitchens require a number of items that don't come into any food category. You will need foil for covering and greaseproof paper or baking parchment for lining baking tins. Some kind of cling wrap will be needed. You can buy ones that are safe to use in the microwave. With all these products that come on a roll, you may as well buy a larger roll, as it rarely takes up much more space, but usually works out cheaper in the long run.

Kitchen paper towel is useful – you can buy one made of recycled paper if you are concerned about the environment. It is best kept in a handy place where it can be instantly grabbed in an emergency – wiping up spilled food colouring on my white kitchen worktops is my favourite. You may also feel that your baking requires bun cases, and cocktail sticks are always useful to have around.

Cleaning

Sadly, not all activities in the kitchen involve preparing and eating food – there is also the inevitable clearing up.

Washing-up liquid has to come first on the list. Experience has taught me that the advertisements are true – you may find a really cheap one, but generally you have to use twice as much of it. It's probably best to invest in a better brand, to ensure that you don't end up with greasy plates and smeary glasses. You may wish to economise by buying a bigger bottle. Personally, I always opt for the small and discreet size. I find the alternative too depressing to contemplate! (You may have gathered by now that the avoidance of washing up is high on my list of priorities!)

You will need dishcloths for mopping up spills and cleaning down surfaces. I feel that the disposable ones are more hygienic, but only if you do dispose of them fairly frequently. A scouring pad will almost certainly be necessary for cleaning pans after the odd culinary disaster (more on these later!), and depending on your washing-up style, you will need a brush or sponge.

Modern ovens often have stay-clean linings, but you will probably still need a can of oven-cleaner in the back of the cupboard. These days, oven-cleaners are very efficient but can give off quite nasty fumes. Always use them with doors and windows open if possible and, if you are asthmatic or prone to chesty coughs, use them cautiously (and if you're not, it's still a pretty good excuse!)

If you are squeamish about plunging your hands into greasy washing-up water, or have nails to die for, buy a pair of rubber gloves. Some people use them when preparing dirty vegetables or cutting up raw meat, but if you want to do this, please buy a separate pair, or you can buy disposable plastic gloves and throw them away after use. Also remember that, unless you have an enormous draining board, a tea-towel or two will be needed. At a pinch, these can double as oven-gloves, though they are obviously not as safe and to do so does reduce their life and good looks! In fact, better buy the oven-gloves, or at least an oven-mit.

A multi-purpose cream or spray kitchen cleaner will save you storing dozens of more specialist bottles. One that includes an anti-bacterial agent is advisable for wiping down worktops and surfaces where you prepare food.

THE BASIC STORE-CUPBOARD

The following list gives suggestions of items that you might like to keep in your store-cupboard, fridge and vegetable rack. This will mean that you always have ingredients to make a decent meal. Of course, nothing is essential, but those items marked with an asterisk (*), although used in several recipes in this book, are certainly optional. If you buy them for the first time when you make a particular recipe, you will have them ready for the next time you need them.

In the store-cupboard

Stock cubes: beef, chicken, vegetable
Cornflour
Salt
Pepper: ground white and black peppercorns (if you have a mill)
Vegetable oil
*Olive oil
*Mustard powder
Flour: plain, self-raising, *wholemeal
*Vanilla essence
*Golden syrup
Sugar: caster, *granulated, *soft brown
Instant coffee
Tea bags
*Cocoa powder
*Rolled oats
Long grain rice
Pasta

*Bicarbonate of soda
*Cream of tartar
*Worcestershire sauce
*Mixed dried fruit
*Walnuts
*Desiccated coconut
Jam
*Ground cinnamon
*Ground ginger
*Chilli powder
Curry paste
Tinned chopped tomatoes
Tinned red kidney beans
Baked beans
Tinned corned beef
Tinned tuna
*Instant mashed potato
Breakfast cereal
UHT skimmed milk
*Tinned rice pudding
*Ready-made long-life custard
Savoury biscuits for cheese

In the vegetable rack

Potatoes: large enough to bake
    (general variety), *King
    Edwards (for roasting)
Onions

Garlic
Apples: eating and *cooking
Oranges

In the refrigerator

Packet of bacon
Packet of ham
Cheddar cheese
Butter
Soft margarine
Tomato purée
*Suet

*Tomatoes
*Celery
*Carrots
*Leeks
*Courgettes
Eggs (or in another cool place)
Milk

Near the sink

Washing-up liquid
Dishcloths
Scouring pad
*Sponge

*Rubber gloves
Oven-cleaner
General-purpose cream or
    liquid cleaner

Anywhere you have space

Cling wrap
Foil
Greaseproof paper or baking
    parchment
*Oven-gloves

Kitchen paper towels
*Bun cases
*Cocktail sticks
Tea-towels

In the freezer

All of these are optional, as you may not have access to a freezer. However, if you do, the following will greatly enhance your store-cupboard.

Garden peas

Pastry: shortcrust, flaky, filo

Minced meat, sausages etc.

Ice cream

Oven chips

Ready-meals

Loaf of sliced bread

Ready-to-bake bread rolls

Breadcrumbs

Tub of raspberries

Cod-in-sauce

Prawns

On the windowsill

Many shops now sell little pots of growing herbs. A couple of these on your kitchen windowsill could be a great asset to your cooking. A few torn basil leaves added to your pasta sauce will be magical. Snipped chives make an excellent garnish.

The list above may look rather discouraging, but these are basic products and you probably already have quite a few of them. As I have stressed in this chapter, cooking and eating are very much a matter of personal choice. If there are things here that you cannot bear, then replace them with something you *do* like.

The real purpose of this chapter is to get you started. If you follow a recipe accurately the first time, you can start experimenting the next time, using what you happen to have to hand. It gives a great feeling of satisfaction to be able to invite unexpected guests to supper, knowing that you can rustle up a quick meal from what you have available.

STORING
FOOD

If you were to listen to some food safety and hygiene experts, you would probably never set foot in a kitchen, but common sense should prevail. Storing food carefully, and as well as the equipment you have allows, is very important. Manufacturers and shops ensure that foods travel the "chill-chain". This means that the manufacturing and packing are done in chilled conditions, the food is transported in chilled lorries and is then stored in the shop at appropriate temperatures. All this care is rather wasted if you then leave the food sitting in a carrier bag in a warm kitchen for several hours.

What are known as "ambient goods" do not need to be chilled. They are perfectly safe stored at room temperature. They may be too dry for bugs to grow, as flour or biscuits are; they may be preserved in sugar or vinegar, as jams and pickles are; or they may have undergone a process involving heat treatment, as canned goods and UHT milk do. To confuse matters further, modern technology is able to produce some goods that look as if they need to be chilled but in fact can be stored at room temperature. These include recipe dishes and some yoghurts and desserts. This is possible as a result of a combination of clever packaging and some heat treatment. Your guide here, as long as you are buying from reputable shops, is that if the dish is not displayed chilled in the store, you do not have to chill it either while the packaging remains intact.

If you do not have access to a fridge, then you will have to shop quite regularly. Butter will survive in a covered container in a cool spot, as will cheese. In fact, ideally cheese is at its best when *not* chilled, but not everyone relishes "essence of stilton" wafting about their kitchen. Fresh meat, fish and poultry *must* be stored chilled or eaten within two or three hours of purchase. If this isn't possible, stick to canned products, such as ham, tuna and corned beef.

It is tempting to argue that our great-grandparents didn't have fridges and didn't have as much food poisoning as we have today either. But houses were built differently then. They usually had a cellar or larder that kept quite cool. Houses themselves, of course, were not so efficiently heated as they are today. Victorian cooks also knew about salting and curing meats and bottling fruits and vegetables as a means of preservation.

Happily, most people today *do* have access to a fridge, although not everyone has a freezer. This is not a problem (unless you have an ice-cream fetish), but it cannot be denied that freezers are very convenient. You can shop in bulk and either freeze the foods at once or make a dish, bolognese sauce, for example, and freeze it in sensible portions. You will then be able to assemble a meal in minutes. I have included a list of useful frozen foods in the buying section (pages 21–52).

Remember that freezing does not kill off bugs, it just makes them very sleepy and slow, so you must only freeze top-quality items. If a piece of meat is reaching the end of its life, popping it in the freezer will certainly not rejuvenate it. While use-by dates are useful for chilled products, they become redundant once that product is frozen. When defrosted, they should be used within 24 hours. Once a product has been frozen and defrosted, it should never be frozen again. Apart from the fact that it may well lose some of its taste and texture, it is a very unsound practice microbiologically. This warning extends to such foods as pastry and cooked rice, as well as the more obvious meat and fish.

Always wrap products securely for the freezer, as they can easily dry out if exposed to the cold air. Meat then suffers from what is called "freezer-burn" – the meat looks bleached and unsightly. It is safe to eat, but may not look particularly appetising. Make sure that you label everything you put in the freezer with its name and date. You may think that this is unnecessary at the time, when it is obvious what the item is and you know when you froze it. Well, months later, when you find a knobbly package, well coated with ice crystals, you will not have a clue whether it is fishcakes or flapjacks. I suspect that we all have to find this out by experience, but you have been warned!

In commercial catering establishments, there are strict rules governing the storage of chilled foodstuffs, which is as it should be. At home, things are different. Not many of us have the facility to keep raw and cooked foods in separate refrigerators, for example. But it is sensible to follow a few basic rules.

1   Always store raw meat, fish and poultry in the bottom of the fridge. This way, drips cannot fall on other foods and contaminate them.

2   Always cover foods carefully. Having special, well-sealed plastic tubs for food is useful, but failing this, use cling wrap that is labelled as being safe for wrapping fatty foods.

3   Never put hot items into the fridge. These will quickly raise the temperature of the entire body of the fridge, which may cause food spoilage and will certainly mean that the motor has to work very hard. Cool cooked products as quickly as possible and then put them into the fridge.

4   As with freezers, try to take what you want from the fridge at one time, so that you are not constantly opening the door. And don't leave the door open while, for example, you are pouring milk into your cup of tea.

5   Do not overfill the fridge. If items are packed tightly, there is not enough room for the cold air to circulate and there may be surfaces that it cannot reach at all.

6   Some fridges have a small icebox at the top. This is handy for making and holding ice-cubes and storing the odd bag of frozen peas, but it is not suitable for long-term storage.

7   If your fridge has a salad drawer (usually at the bottom), use it, as it helps to retain freshness and crispness.

8   Make sure that strong-smelling items are well covered. This is not only true of fish and garlic. I once put a strawberry jelly to set, uncovered, in the fridge. Within hours, I had strawberry-flavoured milk and butter.

9   If they are not auto-defrosters, defrost your fridge and freezer regularly. A large build-up of ice will reduce efficiency. Keep the items you take out as cool as possible while you do this.

10 Try not to exceed the use-by dates on chilled foods, particularly meat and meat products. These have been carefully established to ensure that the product is safe for you to eat.

11 Do not ignore labels that say "refrigerate after opening". Many products no longer contain the preservatives they once did.

12 If you want to store a part-used can of something, tip it into another container. It is tempting just to cover the can and pop it in the fridge, but once opened, the metal can quickly taint the foodstuff.

13 Keep separate chopping boards for raw and cooked foods, particularly meat and poultry.

14 Use a cleaner with an anti-bacterial agent to wipe down surfaces before and after preparing foods.

15 Be ruthless with left-overs. Anything that has been heated should be cooled quickly, covered and kept in the fridge for two days at most. If you haven't eaten it by then, it should be thrown out. Apart from any other health hazards, your fridge will soon be full of little bowls and dishes of tired mashed potato and congealed gravy, which become indistinguishable after a while. So for goodness sake, if you can no longer recognise what it is, don't eat it!

16 When you reheat foods, make sure that they are piping hot right through to the centre. This is particularly important if you are heating something from frozen or if you are using a microwave, which can make food steaming hot in places while it is still frozen solid in others.

A KITCHEN
FOR COOKING

Very few of us have the luxury of being able to design our own kitchens from top to bottom. We often have to cope with fairly basic layouts. Kitchen planners talk grandly about the "work triangle", meaning the distance between the sink, cooker and fridge, which are the three main work areas in a kitchen. There are some common-sense rules in the positioning of these vital items. With luck these have been observed in your kitchen.

1 The cooker should never be placed in a corner of the room. This can make opening the door difficult and also means that you cannot turn pan handles outwards on one side to ensure that they do not hang over an adjoining ring and become dangerously hot.

2 The only thing that should be over the hob is a ventilation hood. Anything else will cause condensation from steaming pans to drop back. If you have low cupboards over a hot chip pan, the dangers are obvious.

3 A cooker should not be placed near a doorway, particularly if it is a busy thoroughfare. You could be taking something hot out of the oven just as somebody rushes through the door. The consequences could be extremely serious.

4 It is nice for a sink to be under a window, as you will have something to look out at when you are washing up, but positioning is largely dictated by the run of the plumbing and is not easily changed.

5 Although fridges are well insulated, it makes their work harder (and uses more electricity) if you put them next to the cooker.

6 An ideal layout is to have your sink and cooker close to each other, with a length of worktop in between and the fridge opposite. This means that you don't have to swerve across to the other side of the kitchen to drain boiling water from pans of vegetables.

A good kitchen design should help to prevent accidents, but still many accidents do occur in the home and the kitchen is a prime site for them. A few simple rules can help prevent minor accidents from turning into disasters.

1 All homes should be protected by a smoke-detector, and this should be situated near, but not actually in, the kitchen. Quite often grilling sausages or other fatty meats causes fat to spit on to the element, resulting in enough smoke to set the alarm beeping. This can be annoying, but remember that the beeping could save your life one day. Flapping a magazine underneath the smoke-detector will soon stop the noise.

2 It is worth keeping a small medicine kit in the kitchen. Antiseptic cream, plasters and burn spray are all that is generally necessary. Burns can be extremely painful. The best approach is to cool down the burnt area as quickly as possible. As long as the skin is not broken or badly blistered, a cooling spray offers immediate relief, but if this is not available, hold the burn under a gently running cold tap for at least 5 minutes.

Cuts always need to be covered when you are cooking. If the cut is clean, rinse it under the cold tap, wipe it dry with a clean cloth or sterile wipe, and cover with a plaster. If there is a danger of infection, apply antiseptic cream before the plaster.

None of this advice is a substitute for professional medical help if you are at all concerned. Once you have dealt with the immediate injury, consider what happened and how you can prevent such an accident in the future.

3 A serious danger in the kitchen is slipping as a result of spills. It is not just fats and oils that can turn the floor into a skating rink. Powders, particularly salt, can make any type of flooring extremely slippery. Egg white is another major culprit. The answer is to clear up any spills as quickly as possible. This is

also true of breakages. Never underestimate how far a sliver of glass can go, or how much glass there is in even the smallest jam jar. The worst mess to clear up is a glass or china container *with* its contents. A jar of runny honey dropped from a reasonable height on to a hard floor was my own triumph in this field. Scooping up as much of the mess as possible, using several layers of newspaper to protect your hands, is the best start, but I can guarantee you'll find sticky patches for weeks to come and you'll need to be careful not to go into the kitchen in bare feet (or allow young children in at all) until you are absolutely sure that every scrap of glass has been retrieved.

Of course, not all accidents in the kitchen happen to people. There's the burnt-on saucepan, the boiled-over milk and the ice-jammed icebox. Never doubt that every cook has endured similar disasters. The secret lies in being able to retrieve them.

Burnt-on saucepans

I'll assume that the pan isn't a non-stick one, in the hope that the disaster would not have happened if it was. Initially, scrape out as much of the burnt food as possible, then soak the whole pan overnight, covering the burnt part with water and a little washing-up liquid. The next day, by attacking it with a scouring pad, you should be able to loosen a lot of the burn. Now give it a good squirt with one of the aerosol cleaners that contain bleach, allow to stand, scour and repeat if necessary. This should eventually clean the pan.

Smelly fridges

This is a surprisingly easy problem to cure. First, remove the offending articles causing the smell. This is often an unpleasant experience, but it has to be done. Then, fill an egg cup or other small container with bicarbonate of soda and leave, uncovered, in the fridge. You will find that this magically absorbs the odour.

Uncleaned ovens

I'm never quite sure how ovens manage to get into the state they do. Nevertheless, sometimes the inevitable must be faced. Lay plenty of newspaper on the floor in front of the cooker and use an oven-cleaner according to the instructions given on the container. I prefer the aerosol type, which sprays a thick foam all over the inside of the cooker. If you use a good-quality cleaner, you should find that it shifts most of the grease. There are two important safety points to be made here. Firstly, do be extremely careful about the fumes, especially if you are asthmatic or have other chest complaints. Secondly, *do* wear rubber gloves. Remember that the cleaner will be vicious with the spills in your cooker. You don't want it doing the same to your hands.

Frozen iceboxes

If you have an icebox at the top of your fridge, you will probably find that it quite quickly literally becomes a box of ice. Very modern fridges have a self-defrosting mechanism, but most of us have to resort to other methods. If you are not able to slip a small bag of frozen peas into your icebox, it is time to defrost. Apart from anything else, it is not good for the motor of your fridge, which has to work extra hard. Remove everything from the fridge, including the shelves, and turn it off. Again, spreading several layers of newspaper over the floor is a wise precaution. Now, you could simply wait for the ice to melt, but this can be a lengthy process. To help it along, fill bowls with boiling water from the kettle and carefully place them under the icebox, and even in it if space permits. Do not be tempted to go out and leave the fridge to it. You would not believe how much water a relatively small amount of ice can turn into. When you have cleared out all the ice, wipe out the fridge with a dry cloth and switch it back on, putting it on its highest setting for a while to ensure that it gets cold as quickly as possible.

COOKING DISASTERS

Most of these are much easier to tackle.

Lumpy sauces

Simply push the sauce through a sieve, using a wooden spoon, rinse out the pan, return the sauce to it and heat through, stirring all the time. You can also sieve mashed potato and batter mixes. If you have an electric mixer or food processor, this may be able to solve the problem for you even more easily.

Spot-welded biscuits

If your biscuits refuse to leave the baking tray, it is probably because they are too cold. Simply return the tray to the oven for one minute and try again.

Sad cakes

If a cake is too brown, rub the finest side of a grater gently over the surface to remove the worst of the burning. A cake that sinks in the middle is usually under-cooked. Simply cut out the middle and brazenly offer it as a ring cake.

Over-seasoning

If you are a little heavy handed with the spices when making a curry or chilli, swirl a little cream or yoghurt into the dish before serving. If you over-salt a casserole, try adding a few slices of raw potato to the dish. The potato absorbs some of the salt as it cooks and can be removed before serving.

Of course, some mistakes cannot be put right. If you over-beat cream, you have butter. Over-cooked vegetables cannot return to crispness, but see page 89 for a recipe to use them up.

USING
THESE RECIPES

The recipes in this book are designed to be as easy as possible to use. They will be even easier if you follow a few basic guidelines.

First, *always* read the recipe all the way through before you start cooking. Check that you have all the ingredients you need (or suitable substitutes), that you fully understand the instructions, and that you have all the equipment used. Having got this far, always follow the recipe step by step. It has been written in a logical order, which will give the best results (and the least washing up!)

You will find a number of symbols at the top of each recipe.

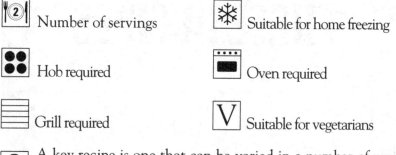

Number of servings   Suitable for home freezing

Hob required   Oven required

Grill required   Suitable for vegetarians

A key recipe is one that can be varied in a number of ways. Most key recipes in this book have suggestions for variations printed after them. It is best to tackle the key recipe first, so that you are confident of the method, before going on to the variations.

Each recipe also has a guide to how long it will take to prepare the dish and then how long it will take to cook it. In the early days, you may find that the preparations take a little longer than stated, but you will soon be up to speed.

In recipes, some phrases and terms are used over and over again. Understanding some of these terms will help you to use other cookbooks as well as this one.

Preheating the oven   The oven is cold when you first turn it on and it takes a while for the cavity to heat up to the temperature you require, probably 15–20 minutes. If you put a potato to bake in a cold oven, nothing disastrous will happen. It will simply take a little longer to cook. When you cook a cake, however, it is important that it goes into a hot oven, so that the raising agents, triggered by the heat, can start to work at once to make the cake light and well risen. If a recipe requires the oven to be preheated, it will say so.

A pinch of an ingredient   This is literally the amount you can pick up between your forefinger and thumb. The phrase is usually applied to spices and seasonings, where only a tiny amount is required.

Flouring worktops   When you are rolling out pastry or biscuit dough, you should always flour the worktop to prevent the dough from sticking. Lightly sprinkle flour from your fingers or a sieve to give a light, even covering to the area that your dough will spread to when rolled out. Sliding a palette knife under the dough will ensure that the flour is doing its job and the dough is not sticking. You should also flour your rolling pin. Simply roll it lightly over your floured worktop before your start working.

Simmering   Quite often a recipe will ask you to bring a liquid to the boil and then simmer for a time. Put the pan and its contents on the highest setting and heat until large bubbles break the surface of the liquid. Then reduce the heat until the liquid is still just bubbling, but the bubbles are smaller and mainly around the edges of the pan. With the lid on, you will achieve a simmer at a lower temperature than with the lid off. Occasionally, a recipe will call for a "fast simmer". This is midway between a gentle simmer and a boil.

The melting method Cakes made using the melting method include flapjacks and gingerbread. Usually the butter and syrup are melted together gently and then the remaining ingredients are stirred in. I'm a great fan of this type of recipe. It is incredibly quick and easy and results in minimal washing up.

Separating eggs Recipes will sometimes just require the yolk or white of an egg, or the whole egg is needed but the white and yolk are added separately. One way of separating the white and yolk is to break the egg carefully into a saucer. Then hold an egg-cup over the yolk and pour the white into a separate bowl. Another method is to crack the egg into two halves over a bowl, twisting one half up quickly to catch the yolk. Pour out any white in the other half into the bowl. Then slide the yolk gently back and forward between the shells, allowing any remaining white to fall away into the bowl beneath as you do so. It is much easier to do than to describe.

Greasing and lining tins To grease a baking tin, simply dip a pastry brush into a bottle of vegetable oil and paint the sides and base of the tin quite lightly. You usually only have to line the base of the tin. Take a piece of greaseproof paper and cut it into roughly the right size by eye. Then push it into the base of the tin, right up to the edges, squeezing it into the corners. Finally, take a small, sharp knife and cut away any excess paper.

Rubbing in This is the method used to make pastry, where fat is rubbed into flour. The flour is put into a bowl first and then the fat is added, cut into small pieces. Dive in with your hands and start squeezing the fat into the flour with your fingers. Try to lift the mixture up as you do this, so that some air is incorporated into the mixture. Gradually, the pieces of fat will become smaller and the mixture will start to look like breadcrumbs. A good test is to shake the bowl gently. Any large remaining pieces of fat will work their way to the top. Carry on working for a bit and then test again.

A level spoonful Scoop out a heaped spoonful of the ingredient and then slide a knife across the top and let the excess fall back into its container. You are left with a level spoonful.

Folding This is one of the most delicate operations in cookery and usually occurs after you have spent a lot of time and energy beating air into something. For some cakes, you beat together eggs and sugar until they are light and fluffy and then fold in the flour. For other dishes, you may need to fold beaten egg whites into a prepared mixture. The process is the same for both. Always use a large metal spoon, which has a finer edge than a wooden spoon. What you are trying to do is to combine the two mixtures, while retaining as many as possible of the air bubbles that you captured during the beating process. Folding is just as the name suggests. You lift up spoonfuls of the mixture and fold them over the top of the rest of the mixture in the bowl. By repeating this, very carefully, until the mixture is evenly blended, you will retain the lightness. Don't be tempted to speed up the process by stirring or beating. You will knock out the air and the dish will become heavy.

Creaming together This phrase is used frequently in cake making and is usually followed by "until light and fluffy". It generally refers to mixing together the fat and sugar in a recipe. If you simply stir these together, the result will be yellow (from the butter or margarine) and quite granular (from the sugar). By beating hard with a wooden spoon, you will soften the fat, begin to dissolve the sugar and mix in air. The mixture will become softer and paler. This task can certainly be done by hand, but an electric mixer makes easy work of it. Creaming is hard to do if the fat has come straight from the fridge, so leave it to soften at room temperature for a while and, unless the recipe specifies butter, use soft margarine. If you have one, you can use a microwave to soften the fat straight from the fridge, but be very careful – you want it to be slightly softened, not melted. This should take only a few seconds. Keep checking every 5 seconds at least.

Adjusting the seasoning to taste This instruction often appears at the end of a recipe. Of course, you should always taste a dish before serving it, particularly if you have guests. If necessary, you can add a little more salt or pepper, but always err on the side of caution. People can add seasoning to their own meal at the table, but it is impossible to take it away once added.

Measuring liquids When a recipe calls for a fluid measure, use a measuring jug. I find it easiest to read the scale of a clear glass or plastic jug. Always place this on a flat surface and lean down so that your eyes are level with the scale before slowly pouring the liquid in. This ensures that you get an accurate measure, which may be essential to the recipe.

Cooling time Some recipes include cooling or chilling time. Don't be tempted to skip this, wherever it comes in the recipe. It is there for a purpose and you ignore it at your peril!

WEIGHTS AND MEASURES

Throughout this book, you will find that recipes are given in metric and imperial measures. Oven temperatures are given for both gas and electric cookers. In case you are not given these alternatives in other cookbooks, the following tables give a rough idea of conversion rates. I have also included a list of abbreviations that you may come across in cookbooks. They can sometimes turn a straightforward recipe into a foreign language!

Remember...

Use metric *or* imperial measures, do not mix both within the same recipe.

Spoon measures are level unless otherwise stated.

The recipes in this books are based on size 3 eggs (sometimes labelled as "medium"), but sizes 2 or 4 will be fine.

Weights

1/2oz	10g	7oz	200g
1oz	25g	8oz	225g
11/2oz	40g	9oz	250g
2oz	50g	10oz	275g
21/2oz	60g	11oz	300g
3oz	75g	12oz	350g
31/2oz	90g	14oz	400g
4oz	110g	1lb	450g
41/2oz	125g	11/2lb	700g
5oz	150g	2lb	900g
6oz	175g	3lb	1.5kg (1500g)

Spoon measures

1/2tspn	2.5ml	2tbspn	30ml
1tspn	5ml	3tbspn	45ml
11/2tspn	7.5ml	4tbspn	60ml
2tspn	10ml	5tbspn	75ml
1tbspn	15ml		

Liquid measures

5 fl oz	$^1/_4$pt	150ml	15 fl oz			425ml
7.5 fl oz		215ml	20 fl oz	1pt		570ml
10 fl oz	$^1/_2$pt	275ml	35 fl oz	$1^3/_4$pt		1 litre

Measurements

$^1/_8$ inch	3mm	$1^1/_2$ inches	4cm
$^1/_4$ inch	5mm	2 inches	5cm
$^1/_2$ inch	1cm	3 inches	7.5cm
$^3/_4$ inch	2cm	4 inches	10cm
1 inch	2.5cm	12 inches	30cm

Oven temperatures

Gas Mark 1	275°F	140°C	Gas Mark 5	375°F	190°C
Gas Mark 2	300°F	150°C	Gas Mark 6	400°F	200°C
Gas Mark 3	325°F	170°C	Gas Mark 7	425°F	220°C
Gas Mark 4	350°F	180°C	Gas Mark 8	450°F	230°C

Abbreviations

oz	ounce	l	litre
lb	pound	fl oz	fluid ounce
g	gram	tspn	teaspoon
kg	kilogram	tbspn	tablespoon
pt	pint	mm	millimetre
ml	millilitre		

SNACKS

RECIPES

SOUPS

GREEN PEA AND BACON CHOWDER

This hearty soup becomes a main meal in a dish when served with crusty bread.

BEAN AND RICE SOUP

Another "big soup", this time suitable for vegetarians too.

STILTON AND LEEK SOUP

A great winter soup, thick and savoury, with the most tantalising smell.

PATES AND DIPS

LEICESTER FISH PATÉ

An unusual combination of fish and cheese that makes a great snack spread on bread or toast.

STILTON DIP

One of those dishes you just cannot stop eating. Try any left-overs spread on hot toast.

EGG DISHES

COOKING EGGS

Perhaps the three greatest snacks: boiled egg with soldiers, scrambled egg on toast and fried egg sandwich.

OMELETTES

A slightly more sophisticated way of serving eggs, with as many variations as your imagination can muster.

EGGY BREAD

This is the childhood snack that everybody forgets, but it is well worth rediscovering.

POTATO AND EGG SAVOURY

Potato slices, cream cheese and hard-boiled eggs, layered in a dish and baked to provide a great supper dish.

SIMPLE SAVOURIES

BUBBLE AND SQUEAK

A great way of using up left-over vegetables and an excellent reason for cooking too many in the first place.

CHEESE SAUCE

Use the basic recipe to make macaroni cheese or to pep up vegetables such as cauliflower or leeks. This is a very useful basic recipe.

FRYING PAN PIZZA

A quick and easy way to make your own pizza, followed by a choice of topping ideas to ring the changes.

STUFFED BAKED POTATOES

The humble potato has now become the basis for one of the most popular snacks around.

TOASTED SANDWICHES

A great snack that you can eat with your fingers and with fillings that are infinitely variable.

WELSH RAREBIT

An extremely superior cheese on toast, well worth the little bit of extra effort.

SAUSAGE ROLL-UPS

Sausages encased in crispy slices of bread, flavoured with mustard – delicious!

GNOCCHI

An Italian dish based on semolina, but bearing absolutely no resemblance to lumpy milk puddings, this is a hearty snack.

BACON CAKES

A cross between scones and wholemeal bread, these savoury cakes should be sampled warm from the oven.

CINNAMON TOAST

A Victorian favourite that is delicious at any time of day.

GREEN PEA AND BACON CHOWDER

This recipe makes a soup so hearty that it is a complete meal when served with fresh, crusty bread. Why not try making your own? The Irish wholemeal bread on page 228 might be a good place to start.

Preparation time: 5 minutes
Cooking time: 40 minutes

You will need:

1 onion, skinned and finely chopped

225g (8oz) streaky bacon, cut into
    rough 2cm (3/4 inch) squares

15ml (1tbspn) vegetable oil

225g (8oz) potatoes, peeled and cut
    into 1cm (1/2 inch) cubes

30ml (2tbspn) plain flour

570ml (20 fl oz) water

2 stock cubes (chicken or vegetable)

570ml (20 fl oz) milk

225g (8oz) frozen peas

50g (2oz) cheddar cheese, grated

Salt and pepper

1 Heat the oil in a large pan over a medium heat. Add the onion and bacon and fry, stirring occasionally, until golden brown – about 10 minutes.

2 Stir in the potato and cook for a further 2 minutes.

3 Stir in the flour and cook for 1 minute. Gradually stir in the water and milk, then add the stock cubes and a pinch of salt and pepper.

4 Turn up the heat and bring to the boil, stirring all the while. Cover the pan, lower the heat and simmer for 15–20 minutes, until the potatoes feel tender when pierced with a sharp knife.

5 Add the peas, return to the boil and simmer, covered, for a further 10 minutes. Serve piping hot, sprinkled with the cheese.

BEAN AND RICE SOUP

This hearty soup, served with crusty bread, would make a tasty supper dish for vegetarian friends.

Preparation time: 15 minutes
Cooking time: 45 minutes

You will need:

45ml (3tbspn) vegetable oil
1 onion, finely chopped
2 cloves garlic, crushed
1 large carrot, peeled and finely chopped
3 stalks celery, finely chopped
400g (14oz) can chopped tomatoes in juice
570ml (20fl oz) water
2 vegetable stock cubes

400g (14oz) can red kidney beans,
    drained and rinsed
110g (4oz) long grain rice
5ml (1tspn) mixed dried herbs
30ml (2tbspn) finely chopped fresh parsley
Salt and pepper
Pinch of caster sugar

1 Heat the oil in a large saucepan over a medium heat. Add the onion, garlic, carrot and celery and cook, stirring occasionally, for 10 minutes.

2 Add the tomatoes and their juice, water and stock cubes, cover and simmer for 10 minutes.

3 Add the beans, rice, dried herbs, parsley, pinch of salt, pepper and sugar. Simmer gently for 15–20 minutes, or until the rice is cooked. Serve piping hot.

Cook's Tip

If you have a liquidiser, blend half the mixture at the end of stage 2, then proceed with the rest of the recipe. This will give you a thicker and creamier soup.

STILTON AND LEEK SOUP

This is a seriously warming soup, the kind to come home to after a bracing winter's walk. You don't need a liquidiser to make this recipe, but I can't deny that it makes life a lot easier.

Preparation time: 10 minutes
                              + puréeing time
Cooking time: 25 minutes

You will need:

25g (1oz) butter

700g (1¹/₂lb) leeks, trimmed and
    thinly sliced

1 large potato, about 225–275g (8–10oz),
    cut into 1cm (¹/₂ inch) cubes

570ml (20 fl oz) water

2 vegetable stock cubes

110g (4oz) stilton cheese, grated
    (with rind cut off)

Salt and pepper

150ml (5 fl oz) single cream

1 Melt the butter in a large saucepan over a medium to high heat. Add the leeks and potato and stir about in the butter for a couple of minutes. This process is known as "sweating" the vegetables and helps to bring out their flavour.

2 Add the water and stock cubes to the pan, bring to the boil, then reduce the heat to medium and simmer for about 15 minutes, until the potatoes feel very tender when pierced with a sharp knife.

3 If you have a liquidiser, simply throw in the vegetables and stock (you will probably need to do this in two batches) and blend until smooth. If you do not have a liquidiser or food processor, you will need to push the mixture through a sieve resting over a large bowl. Either way, once you have your purée, return it to the saucepan and stir in the stilton cheese and salt and pepper to taste.

4 Stir over a medium heat until the cheese has melted and the soup is piping hot.

5 Just before serving, stir in the cream.

Cook's Tip

If you do not have any cream, you could use half milk and half stock in the basic recipe, or you could stay with all stock and add a little more stilton – the cream is just to add richness. If your stilton is very ripe, grating may be difficult, so just throw it into the purée in lumps – it will soon melt.

LEICESTER FISH PATÉ

This is a quick and easy recipe for a delicious paté that makes an excellent light lunch, served with crusty bread and fresh tomatoes, or an elegant first course at a dinner party, accompanied by crisp, warm toast.

Preparation time: 15 minutes
+ chilling time

You will need:
185g (6¹/₂oz) can tuna in oil or brine, drained
200g (7oz) Leicester cheese, grated as finely as possible
10ml (2tspn) lemon juice
150ml (5 fl oz) carton natural yoghurt
30ml (2tbspn) chopped fresh parsley
Salt and pepper

1 Place the tuna in a large bowl and mash with a fork to break up the chunks. Add the cheese and lemon juice and mix well.

2 Beat in the yoghurt and parsley with a wooden spoon and add salt and pepper to taste.

3 Pile the mixture into a large serving dish or on to individual plates and chill for at least two hours.

STILTON DIP

Dips make great snacks when you are having friends round. You can nibble them over a long period of time and they are much more exciting than a bowl of peanuts. Try to find a nice ripe piece of stilton for a good flavour and ease of creaming.

Preparation time: 20 minutes

You will need:

225g (8oz) stilton cheese

225ml (8 fl oz) mayonnaise

45ml (3tbspn) milk

Black pepper

3 stalks celery

1 red skinned apple

1 green skinned apple

Lemon juice

110g (4oz) seedless green grapes

110g (4oz) seedless black grapes

Little cocktail biscuits

1 Cut any rind away from the cheese and place the stilton in a bowl. Mash it with a fork to break it up.

2 Add the mayonnaise to the bowl and beat with a wooden spoon until you get a creamy, fairly smooth mixture. Beat in the milk and add pepper to taste.

3 Scrape the dip into a bowl and place it in the centre of a large plate.

4 Cut the celery into sticks about 7.5 x 1cm (3 x 1/2 inch). Cut the apples into quarters, cut away the cores and cut each quarter into thick slices – you should get 3 or 4 slices from each quarter. Place the slices in a bowl, add 15ml (1tbspn) of lemon juice and toss the apple about so that all the slices get coated in the juice. Remove the stalks from the grapes, wash them and pat them dry with kitchen paper.

5 Now arrange the celery, apple slices and grapes on the plate, surrounding the bowl of dip. Place the biscuits in a separate bowl so that they keep their crispness.

COOKING EGGS

Eggs have been described as nature's convenience food. They have many uses in cookery: to give a shiny surface to baked foods, to bind ingredients together, to hold bubbles of air in a mixture to add lightness, and to enable a liquid to set when cooked, to name but a few. They are also the base of many excellent snacks. I've included even the most simple forms below because they are often appallingly badly cooked. How *long* you like your eggs cooked is largely a matter of personal taste, but the guides below will give you a starting point.

BOILED EGGS

1 Leave the eggs at room temperature for a couple of hours before cooking.

2 Fill a small pan to a depth of about 4cm (1½ inches) with cold water.

3 Place on a hob on a high heat until the water is boiling.

4 Using a slotted spoon, carefully lower as many eggs as required into the water, reducing the heat slightly so that the water is gently bubbling around the eggs, and start timing.

5 Soft-boiled eggs can be cooked from 3 to 5 minutes, depending on how you like them. A three-minute egg leaves the white quite runny, while at five minutes, the yolk will have begun to set. Somewhere in between suits most people. Of course, larger eggs do take slightly longer to cook than smaller ones. With practice, you will be able to judge this quite easily.

TOAST SOLDIERS

1 Put the grill on to its highest setting as soon as you put the pan on the stove.

2 As soon as the timer is on for the eggs, slip the bread under the grill. Cook until golden brown, then turn over and grill the other side.

3 You should have enough time to butter the toast and cut it into fingers before the eggs are cooked.

SCRAMBLED EGGS

1 Break the eggs into a measuring jug, allowing about two per person. Add a good pinch of salt and pepper and 15ml (1tbspn) of milk for each egg. Whisk together until the mixture is quite smooth.

2 Now put about 10g (¹/₂oz) of butter per two eggs in a pan (a non-stick one is a good idea here) over a low heat and allow it to melt.

3 Pour in the eggs and start stirring gently with a wooden spoon. What will happen is that the eggs start cooking on the base of the pan, where it is hottest. The idea is to scrape them away and let the raw egg take the place of the cooked egg. By continually stirring and repeating this process, you will get scrambled eggs. Here again you can choose how well you want them cooked, whether creamy or very well cooked. Bear in mind that the eggs will continue to cook on the base of the pan even when it is off the heat, so serve them up quickly, or take them off the hob when they are slightly underdone.

Cook's Tip

Put the pan in water to soak as soon as you can. It cannot be denied that a scrambled-egg pan is a swine to clean.

TOAST FOR SCRAMBLED EGGS

Turn the grill on to its highest setting as soon as you put the pan on the stove and slip the bread under as soon as you start to cook the eggs, remembering to turn it over after a minute or so.

FRIED EGGS

1 Heat about 30ml (2tbspn) of vegetable oil in a frying pan over a high heat.

2 Crack an egg into a cup, being careful not to break the yolk, and slide this into the hot fat. Be careful: the hot fat may spit a little.

3 As the egg begins to cook, the white will turn opaque. Spoon a little of the hot fat over the thickest part of the white and the yolk to help it to cook. If you like your eggs "over easy", flip the egg over with a fish slice or palette knife when it is nearly cooked and fry for a few more seconds. My ideal fried egg has a lacy brown and crispy edge, a softly set white and a runny yolk – you may have other ideas! Try popping the cooked egg between two slices of buttered bread for a wickedly good fried-egg sandwich. (It's best to eat this with a knife and fork – picking it up and biting could prove very messy!)

OMELETTES

Omelettes are one of the greatest snack dishes for speed, convenience and versatility. With a variety of fillings, they can be as plain or as exotic as you like. Served with a green salad, they make an excellent lunch or supper dish. The following recipe is for one person. You can make one larger or several smaller omelettes if you are catering for a crowd, and as they are quick to cook, being a one-frying-pan household is no problem.

Preparation time: 5 minutes
Cooking time: 5 minutes

You will need:
3 eggs
15ml (1tbspn) milk
Salt and pepper
Oil for cooking

1 Whisk the eggs with the milk until well blended and broken down. Add a good pinch of salt and pepper and mix again.

2 Heat 15ml (1tbspn) of oil in a frying pan over a medium to high heat. Pour in all the egg mixture.

3 Now get to work with a wooden spatula, pulling the omelette away from the edge of the pan as it cooks and allowing the runny mixture to run into its place. This also adds texture to the omelette, giving it a rippled effect. It is up to you how long you cook the omelette – some people prefer them soft in the middle, while others like them nice and firm.

4 When it is ready, slide the omelette on to a serving plate. When it is halfway out, flip the pan forward so that the omelette folds in half. This takes practice, but the omelette will taste just as good if it falls out of the pan in a heap!

You can add almost anything to an omelette, either as a filling, or cooked in the pan before the eggs are added. Here are a few quick and easy ideas.

HERB OMELETTE

You will need:
Omelette recipe (page 85)
About 15ml (1tbspn) of chopped herbs, such as parsley, sage and chives

Add the herbs to the beaten egg mixture and stir in well before cooking.

CHEESE OMELETTE

You will need:
Omelette recipe (page 85)
40g (1^1/2oz) cheddar cheese, grated

Turn the grill to its highest setting before you start cooking. When the omelette is nearly cooked, sprinkle over the cheese, take the pan off the hob and slide it under the grill (keeping the handle away from the heat) until the cheese melts. Serve as before.

MUSHROOM AND GARLIC OMELETTE

You will need:
Omelette recipe (page 85)
30ml (2tbspn) vegetable oil
40g (1^1/2oz) button mushrooms, sliced
Clove of garlic, crushed

Heat the oil in the pan over a medium to high heat. Add the mushrooms and garlic and fry for about 3–4 minutes, stirring well. Add the beaten egg and proceed as for the main recipe.

EGGY BREAD

Sometimes known as French toast, this is a quick and easy snack that can be eaten on its own, with grilled bacon or (omitting the salt and pepper) drizzled with golden syrup.

Preparation time: 5 minutes
Cooking time: 10 minutes

You will need:

1 small, unsliced white loaf, not too crusty	Salt and pepper
150ml (5 fl oz) milk	Oil for frying
3 eggs	

1 Cut the loaf into slices about 2cm (³/4 inch) thick.

2 In a bowl, mix together the eggs and milk and add a good pinch of salt and pepper. Pour this mixture into a fairly shallow dish.

3 Place a slice of bread in the milk mixture, leave it for 30 seconds, then turn it over and leave for another 30 seconds. Remove the slice to a plate and repeat with the remaining bread. This should use up all the egg and milk mixture.

4 In the meantime, heat 30ml (2tbspn) of oil in a frying pan over a medium to high heat. Add the first slice of dipped bread, cook until golden on the base, then flip over with a palette knife or fish slice and brown the other side. Keep warm on a plate, perhaps under a low grill, while cooking the other slices.

POTATO AND EGG SAVOURY

This dish makes quite a substantial snack. It is ideal if you have some left-over boiled potatoes lurking in the fridge.

Preparation time: 35 minutes + cooling
Cooking time: 25 minutes

You will need:

700g (1¹/₂lb) potatoes	Salt and pepper
4 eggs	60ml (4tbspn) milk
110g (4oz) cream cheese with chives	25g (1oz) butter

1 Peel the potatoes, place in a pan and cover with water. Add 5ml (1tspn) of salt and place on a high heat. Bring to the boil and simmer for 15 minutes. Drain and cool slightly. You want the potatoes to be nearly cooked but still slightly hard.

2 Meanwhile, hard boil the eggs. Put a small pan, half full of water, on a high heat and bring to the boil. Place the eggs, one at a time, on a spoon and lower them into the water. Boil gently for 10 minutes, then quickly pour off the boiling water and fill the pan with cold water. This will cool the eggs and stop a grey ring from forming between the yolk and the white.

3 When cool enough to handle, slice the potatoes. Then remove the shells from the eggs and slice them too.

4 Generously butter an ovenproof dish and cover the base with about a third of the potato slices. Spread half the cheese over the potato slices, then cover with half the egg slices. Sprinkle with salt and pepper. Repeat the layers, finishing with a final topping of potato slices. Pour the milk over and dot with little pieces of butter.

5 Bake in an oven preheated to 200°C/400°F/Gas Mark 6 for 20–25 minutes, until piping hot with a crispy, golden top.

BUBBLE AND SQUEAK

This is a great dish for using up left-overs, but it is too good to wait until you happen to have some cold mashed potato and cooked cabbage lurking in your fridge, so this recipe starts from basics.

Preparation time: 35 minutes
Cooking time: 20 minutes

  V

You will need:

450g (1lb) potatoes
Salt and pepper
350g (12oz) green cabbage
   or brussels sprouts

25g (1oz) butter
45ml (3tbspn) milk
30ml (2tbspn) vegetable oil

1 Peel the potatoes and cut them into evenly sized chunks. Put in a saucepan, cover with cold water, add 5ml (1tspn) salt and place on the hob on a high heat. Bring to the boil, then reduce the heat and simmer the potatoes for about 20 minutes, or until they feel tender when pierced with a sharp knife. Drain.

2 Meanwhile, finely shred the cabbage or trim the sprouts (see page 112) and cook in boiling water, with 5ml (1tspn) of salt added, for 12–15 minutes. Although I would normally suggest cooking cabbage and sprouts until still slightly crisp, they need to be quite well cooked for this recipe, so they will mash down and combine with the potato. When cooked, drain.

3 Mash the potatoes with a masher or fork until smooth. Add the butter and milk and mix well. Now add the cabbage or sprouts and mix together well, slightly breaking them down. Add a pinch of salt and lots of pepper.

4 Heat the oil in a frying pan over a medium heat. Add the potato mixture and press down well to form an even layer over the base of the pan. Cook for about 10 minutes, until a brown "crust" has developed on the base. (Investigate by pulling up the side with a palette knife.)

5 Cut into four wedges, turn them over with the aid of a palette knife and cook for a further 8–10 minutes. Sometimes a bubble and squeak works well and you can serve up four beautiful pieces, nicely browned top and bottom. At other times it refuses to be helpful and you end up with a messy mound. Never mind, it will still taste good, served, perhaps, with a dollop of brown sauce and some grilled bacon or cold ham.

CHEESE SAUCE

This recipe includes an easy way of making a basic white sauce. You can then turn this into a rich cheese sauce, which in turn can become a number of supper dishes. By varying the amount of cornflour, you can adjust the thickness of the sauce.

Preparation time: 5 minutes
Cooking time: 10 minutes

You will need:

570ml (20 fl oz) full cream milk
30ml (2tbspn) cornflour
2.5ml (1/2tspn) mustard powder

Salt and pepper
175g (6oz) mature cheddar cheese, grated

1 Place the cornflour, mustard powder and a pinch of salt and pepper in a measuring jug and mix to a paste with about 75ml (5tbspn) of the milk.

2 Put the rest of the milk in a small pan over a high heat. When small bubbles start to form around the side of the pan, take it off the heat and pour it over the cornflour, stirring well.

3 Give the mixture a final brisk stir and return it to the pan over a medium to high heat. Bring the mixture to the boil, stirring all the time. As the mixture gets hotter, it will start to thicken and the stirring will stop lumps from forming. Try to stir in a figure-of-eight pattern, which will cover the base of the pan better than stirring round and round. When the sauce is thickened, cook it, still stirring, for a further minute. This will ensure that the starch in the cornflour is fully activated.

4 Remove the pan from the heat, add the cheese and stir until it has melted. Taste and adjust the seasoning if necessary.

MACARONI CHEESE

You will need:
Cheese sauce recipe (page 91)
225g (8oz) macaroni
5ml (1tspn) salt
50g (2oz) cheddar cheese, grated

1 Place the macaroni in a large pan of boiling water with the salt. Bring to the boil, then reduce the heat and simmer until the macaroni is cooked (about 10–12 minutes), stirring once or twice to ensure that the macaroni pieces do not stick together.

2 Drain the macaroni and put in a large, ovenproof dish. Pour the cheese sauce over, mix well and sprinkle with the grated cheddar cheese.

3 Bake in an oven preheated to 200°C/400°F/Gas Mark 6 for 15–25 minutes, depending on whether you have put it in the oven at once or have allowed the pasta and sauce to become cold before reheating. The dish should be served piping hot with the cheese on top melted and golden brown.

CAULIFLOWER CHEESE

You will need:
Cheese sauce recipe (page 91)
1 large cauliflower
Salt
50g (2oz) cheddar cheese, grated

Trim the cauliflower into even-sized florets and cook in boiling salted water for 10–12 minutes (see page 113). Drain and proceed as for macaroni cheese.

FRYING PAN PIZZA

This is one of the quickest and easiest ways of making a pizza. The recipe below is for the basic base, followed by a number of ideas for toppings.

Preparation time: 10 minutes
Cooking time: 15 minutes

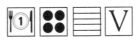

You will need:
110g (4oz) plain flour
Pinch of salt
5ml (1tspn) baking powder
60ml (4tbspn) cold water
45ml (3tbspn) vegetable oil

1 Sift the flour, salt and baking powder into a bowl. Add the water and work together to make a firm dough.

2 Turn the dough out on to a floured work-surface and shape into a 17.5cm (7 inch) round. This does not have to be too accurate – don't worry if the edges are a bit ragged.

3 Heat the oil in a frying pan over a medium heat. Add the pizza base and cook for 5 minutes, then turn over. The easiest way to do this is to slide the pizza on to a plate, place another plate on top and turn the plates over. The cooked side of the pizza should now be uppermost. Slide it back into the pan. Now is the time to add the topping, while the base finishes cooking – about 8–10 minutes.

4 Have the grill preheated to high and slide the pan under, to melt the cheese and heat the topping. Serve at once.

TOPPINGS

1 Drain a 400g (14oz) can of chopped tomatoes in natural juice into a sieve – you do not need the juice. Turn the tomatoes into a bowl, add a pinch of Italian seasoning, salt and pepper to taste and 15ml (1tbspn) of tomato purée and mix well.

2 Grate 75g (3oz) of cheddar cheese. For the most basic pizza, spread the tomato mixture over the cooked top surface of the pizza, sprinkle with the grated cheese and leave until the underside of the base is cooked.

3 Flash under the preheated grill until the cheese is golden and bubbling. Serve at once.

VARIATIONS

Add finely sliced mushrooms over the tomato sauce.

Add drained and flaked canned tuna, chopped ham, or salami slices between the tomato and cheese.

Use thin slices of mozzarella instead of the grated cheddar cheese.

Serve, cut into wedges, as ideal finger-food for a buffet party.

STUFFED BAKED POTATOES

A steaming baked potato, with crisp skin and a fluffy middle, a lump of butter melting on top, is a fine thing. But scooping out the flesh, mixing it with other ingredients and piling it back into the shell makes a good thing even better. Below are some suggestions, but your imagination is really the only limit. A side-order of baked beans turns these recipes into filling meals.

Preparation time: 10–15 minutes
Cooking time: 1¹/₂ hours + reheating

You will need:
Large, evenly-sized potatoes (one for each person), with no obvious blemishes, weighing about 225–275g (8–10oz) each

1 Cut a slit all around the middle of each potato, about 3mm (¹/₈ inch) deep. This makes it easy to halve the cooked potato and will also prevent the potato from bursting in the hot oven.

2 Place the potatoes on a baking tray in an oven preheated to 180°C/350°F/Gas Mark 4 for about 1¹/₂ hours, or until they feel tender when you insert a sharp knife through the slit. Baked potatoes are very well behaved and if you already have the oven on they will accommodate most cooking temperatures, although the cooking time may vary.

3 Remove the potatoes from the oven and cut in half through the slit. Hold the hot potato in a clean tea-towel to protect your hands and start to scoop out the flesh into a bowl. I find a dessertspoon is the best tool for this. Remember to try to keep the skins intact.

4 Mash the potato with a fork or potato-masher until smooth and blend with one of the fillings suggested below.

5 Pile the mixture back into the shells, remembering that it will be well mounded up with the additional ingredients included.

6 Return the potato halves to the oven for about 20 minutes, until piping hot and flecked brown on top.

FILLINGS

Mix 75g (3oz) of grated cheddar cheese with the potato – simple but very good. You can spruce this up by adding a few chopped chives or spring onions.

Drain a small can of tuna in oil, mash into small chunks and mix with the potato. Some may argue that a small, finely chopped onion improves this filling.

In a small pan, fry a couple of rashers of finely chopped bacon in 5ml (1tspn) of oil over a medium heat for 3 minutes. Add 25g (1oz) of sliced button mushrooms and cook for a further 3 minutes. Mix with the potato.

Defrost and drain about 75g (3oz) of cooked prawns. Mix into the potato with 15ml (1tbspn) of soft cheese and a pinch of chopped fresh parsley.

VARIATIONS

Instead of scooping out the middle of the potato, you can just dollop a filling on top of the potato half and serve it at once. Grated cheese and pickle, tuna or prawn and mayonnaise, and cottage cheese with sweetcorn all work well.

TOASTED SANDWICHES

These have to be one of the most versatile snacks and you don't need a fancy sandwich-maker – as long as you have a grill, you are in business.

HAM AND CHEESE TOASTED SANDWICH

Preparation time: 5–10 minutes
Cooking time: 5 minutes

You will need:
2 slices of bread
25g (1oz) cheddar cheese, grated
1 slice of ham
Mustard

1 Preheat the grill to high and arrange the rack so that there is space for a filled sandwich.

2 Place one slice of bread under the grill and toast until golden brown. Turn over. Cover evenly with the grated cheese and return to the heat until the cheese just melts and bubbles.

3 Cover the cheese with the ham (processed, square ham is ideal), and flash under the grill for 30 seconds, to heat the ham.

4 Spread mustard on one side of the remaining slice of bread and place this, mustard side down, on top of the ham. Return to the grill and toast until golden. Serve at once.

VARIATION

Replace the ham with a sliced tomato or 15ml (1tbspn) of pickle. If you are feeling anti-social, you could add a few thin slices of raw onion.

TUNA AND SWEETCORN SANDWICH

You will need:

2 slices of bread

1 small can tuna, drained

15ml (1tbspn) canned sweetcorn kernels, drained

15ml (1tbspn) mayonnaise

1 Mash the tuna up in a bowl and add the sweetcorn and mayonnaise. Spread this evenly over one slice of bread and top with the other.

2 Preheat the grill to high. Place the sandwich under the grill and toast until the top is golden brown. Turn over and repeat. Serve at once.

BACON AND TOMATO SANDWICH

You will need:

2 slices of bread

3 rashers of streaky bacon

1 tomato

15ml (1tbspn) mayonnaise

1 Cook the bacon under a high grill for about 3 minutes on each side until crispy. Slice the tomato.

2 Arrange the bacon slices over one piece of bread and top with the tomato slices. Place under the grill for 2 minutes.

3 Cover the tomato with the other slice of bread, return to the grill and toast until the top is golden brown. Turn over and toast the other side.

4 Lift the top slice of toast, smear the mayonnaise over the bacon, return the "lid" and serve at once.

WELSH RAREBIT

This may seem like a lot of effort to make cheese on toast, but this is a seriously superior product. Sadly, it requires 60ml (4tbspn) of brown ale – goodness knows what you can do with the rest of the bottle!

Preparation time: 10 minutes
Cooking time: 5 minutes

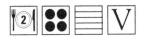

10g (1/2oz) butter
15ml (1tbspn) plain flour
30ml (2tbspn) milk
60ml (4tbspn) brown ale
10ml (2tspn) Worcestershire sauce

2.5ml (1/2tspn) mustard powder
Good pinch of salt and pepper
225g (8oz) cheddar cheese, grated
4 thick slices of bread
Butter for bread

1 Melt the butter in a pan over a medium heat until runny. Remove from the heat and stir in the flour to give a thick, smooth paste.

2 Now slowly add the milk and ale, mixing well after each addition, keeping the sauce as smooth as possible. Mix in the Worcestershire sauce, mustard powder, and salt and pepper.

3 Return the pan to a low heat and cook, stirring all the time, for 2–3 minutes, until the sauce thickens. Vigorous stirring will usually get rid of any lumps. Turn the grill to high.

4 Mix in the cheese and cook, stirring, for another minute, until melted.

5 Toast the bread on each side and butter generously. Divide the cheese mixture between the toast slices, spreading it right to the edges.

6 Return to the grill and cook for 3–4 minutes until the topping is golden brown with a few darker patches. Serve at once.

SAUSAGE ROLL-UPS

These make a very tasty snack, almost a main meal if you serve them with baked beans or a salad. They also make a good savoury course for high tea.

Preparation time: 25 minutes
Cooking time: 15 minutes

You will need:
225g (8oz) thin pork sausages (should equal 8 sausages)
8 slices of thinly sliced white bread
English mustard
Butter (at room temperature)
Cocktail sticks

1 First cook the sausages as directed on the packet. I would suggest that you grill them as this gets rid of excess fat.

2 Meanwhile cut the crusts off the bread. Spread with butter on one side then turn over and spread the other side thinly with mustard.

3 Now place a sausage at one corner of the mustard side and roll up to the other corner. Secure by pushing a cocktail stick through. Repeat to use all the bread and the sausages. Place on a baking tray.

 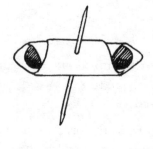

4 Cook in an oven preheated to 200°C/400°F/Gas Mark 6 for about 15 minutes, until the outside is golden and crispy.

VARIATION

Replace the mustard with yeast extract spread, tomato ketchup or pickle.

GNOCCHI

This is the basic recipe for gnocchi, a traditional Italian dish. You can now buy a whole range of pasta sauces to heat and serve with the gnocchi, but for a snack, it is delicious as below, sprinkled with cheese and grilled until golden brown and sizzling.

Preparation time: 15 minutes + cooling
Cooking time: 10 minutes

You will need:
275ml (10 fl oz) milk
50g (2oz) semolina
170g (6oz) cheddar cheese, grated
5ml (1tspn) salt
Pinch of cayenne pepper (optional)
Pinch of ground nutmeg (optional)
Vegetable oil

1 Place the milk in a saucepan (preferably a non-stick one) over a medium heat. When the milk is beginning to bubble around the edges, turn the heat to high and shoot in all the semolina at once. Stir very vigorously. The mixture will thicken rapidly, but keep cooking and stirring for 2 minutes.

2 Remove the pan from the heat and stir in half the grated cheese and the seasonings. Brush a large plate with a little oil and turn out the semolina mix on to this. Spread out evenly, to about 1cm ($^1/_2$ inch) thick and leave until cold.

3 When cold, cut the gnocchi into 2.5cm (1 inch) squares and arrange, slightly overlapping, in an oiled, shallow ovenproof dish. Sprinkle evenly with the remaining cheese.

4 Preheat the grill to medium, slide the dish under it and heat until the cheese is bubbling and golden brown and the gnocchi heated through.

BACON CAKES

For a really delicious snack, try to serve these bacon cakes still warm from the oven, split open and spread with butter. They also make an excellent accompaniment to soup.

Preparation time: 30 minutes + cooling
Cooking time: 25 minutes

You will need:

8 rashers streaky bacon

225g (8oz) self-raising flour

25g (1oz) butter

75g (3oz) cheddar cheese, grated

150ml (5 fl oz) milk

15ml (1tbspn) tomato ketchup

10ml (2tspn) Worcestershire sauce

Vegetable oil

1 First grill the bacon as instructed on the packet and allow to cool. Cut into 1cm ($^1/_2$ inch) squares.

2 Sift the flour into a bowl. Add the butter and rub the butter and flour between your fingers until no large lumps remain. Stir in the bacon and 60g ($2^1/_2$oz) of the cheese.

3 Mix together the milk, tomato ketchup and Worcestershire sauce in a small bowl and add to the flour mix to make a soft dough, kneading gently so that it comes together in a ball.

4 Turn the dough on to a floured worktop and roll it into a 20cm (8 inch) circle. Carefully lift it on to a lightly oiled baking tray and cut through into 8 wedges, but do not separate. Brush with a little milk if wished and sprinkle with the reserved cheese.

5 Bake in an oven preheated to 200°C/400°F/Gas Mark 6 for 25 minutes, until slightly risen and golden. Remove from the oven and pull the wedges apart while still warm.

CINNAMON TOAST

This is a wickedly good and incredibly quick snack, delicious for breakfast, morning coffee or afternoon tea. It really must be made with butter for the best results.

Preparation time: 5 minutes
Cooking time: 5 minutes

6 slices of bread – thickly sliced is preferable, and brown, white or even malted tea
    bread all work well.
50g (2oz) butter, at room temperature
110g (4oz) soft brown sugar
10ml (2tspn) ground cinnamon

1 In a small bowl, beat together the butter, sugar and cinnamon until well mixed and of a spreadable consistency.

2 Preheat the grill to high, place the bread under the grill and toast on one side only.

3 Remove the bread from the grill, turn over so that the untoasted side is uppermost and divide the butter mix between the slices. Spread out to cover the bread right to the edges and corners.

4 Return the bread, buttered side up, to the grill and toast until the topping just starts to caramelise. Cut each slice across from corner to corner each way to make 4 small triangles and serve quickly, while still hot.

SALADS
and
VEGETABLES

RECIPES

SAGE DERBY LAYER

This delicious recipe is too good to use as an accompaniment. It makes a substantial supper or lunch dish.

POTATOES O'BRIEN

This delicious potato dish will enhance any meal. Try it with cold meats or casseroles at a casual supper or elegant dinner party.

BRAISED RED CABBAGE

Anyone who has doubts about the deliciousness of cabbage should try this dish – it makes winters worth waiting for!

COLESLAW

The recipe given is just a start – adapt and add to it to make your own special salad.

STUFFED MARROW

Here is a wonderful way to serve what can be a rather bland vegetable. Once you have tried this filling, experiment with your own version.

RATATOUILLE

A classic dish, using Mediterranean vegetables, ratatouille can be eaten hot or cold, as a starter or accompaniment. A truly versatile dish!

BUYING AND USING VEGETABLES

The following pages give a guide to buying, preparing and cooking some of the more common vegetables. With modern distribution techniques, many once seasonal vegetables are now available all year round, although there may still be certain parts of the year when they are more plentiful, better quality and cheaper.

Supermarkets now make life easier by providing ready prepared vegetables – sliced courgettes, trimmed sprouts, shelled peas and even shredded cabbage, but, of course, you pay a price for this convenience and nothing will beat the flavour of a pea freshly popped from its shell.

Some shops offer the choice of organically grown vegetables, where no artificial fertilisers or pesticides have been used in their cultivation. These tend to be more expensive than their non-organic counterparts. It is your decision whether you think the extra cost is worthwhile, but in either case it is advisable to wash all vegetables before you cook or eat them.

It is often more convenient to buy vegetables from the supermarket when you are doing the rest of your shopping, rather than visiting a specialist greengrocer. Since you may only visit the supermarket once a week, it is vital that you store your vegetables correctly. Most stores offer a serve-yourself policy, where you select and bag up your own choice of each vegetable, before having it weighed and priced at the checkout. This means that you can select the freshest looking specimens. You can check that your cabbage has a firm heart, select courgettes of similar sizes for even cooking, and buy just one leek if that is all you need.

Following the basic information below are some suggestions for more exciting ways of serving vegetables, some of which almost become a meal in their own right. If you are cooking for one, it sometimes seems too much bother to cook a selection of vegetables, but they play an important part in a healthy and balanced diet and anyway, they are delicious, so do try to make the most of them. If you are put off by youthful memories of slimy spinach and grey cabbage, then you will welcome the modern approach to cooking vegetables, which retains their crunch and colour.

Many vegetables can be cooked in boiling water. A basic guide is as follows:

Above the ground: put into boiling water
Below the ground: put into cold water

The exceptions are baby carrots and new potatoes, which should also be placed in boiling water. If your grasp of basic botany isn't too strong, don't worry. You cannot do much harm by putting everything into boiling water.

For the "above-the-ground" vegetables, proceed as follows. Half fill a pan with cold water and add 2.5ml ($\frac{1}{2}$tspn) of salt. Cover and place on the hob on a high setting and bring to the boil. Add the prepared vegetables (carefully, because splashes will be hot), re-cover the pan and leave on high to return to the boil. When the water is bubbling again, reduce the heat to low and simmer for the time suggested on the following pages.

For "below-the-ground" vegetables, the method is even simpler. Place the prepared vegetables in a pan and just cover with cold water. Add 2.5ml (1/2tspn) of salt and cover. Place the pan on the hob on a high setting and bring to the boil. Reduce the heat to low and simmer for the time suggested on the following pages.

If hob space is short, there is no reason why you should not cook a couple of vegetables together, as long as they have similar cooking times. Broccoli and cauliflower florets, or sliced carrots and celery, are examples that work well.

Aubergine

I always feel that aubergines should have a stronger flavour than they do, looking so rich and majestic with their plump and shiny purple skins. In fact, their flavour is subtle and their texture unusual.

Available: All year round.

Storage: Keep in the refrigerator.

Preparation: Wipe the skin but do not peel. Trim off the stalk end. Cut into 1cm (1/2 inch) slices just before using, as the flesh discolours quite quickly. However, don't worry if the flesh does turn brown, it will still taste just as good.

Cooking: Aubergine is delicious fried in a little hot oil for 2–3 minutes on each side.

Other uses: Try dicing aubergine and adding it to a vegetable curry. It is an essential ingredient in classic moussaka and delicious in ratatouille (see page 133).

Broad beans

The large beans snuggle in a furry pod. They have a greyish outer skin, which can be eaten or popped off after cooking to reveal the bright green inner bean.

Available: April to September.

Storage: Keep in a cool place.

Preparation: Broad bean shells do not pop like pea pods, so you have to twist and tear them open to be able to scoop out the beans.

Cooking: Cook in boiling salted water for 15 minutes. Drain and serve.

Other uses: Broad beans are classically served with a parsley sauce poured over them.

French beans

These are little, round, green beans about 7.5–15cm (3–6 inches) long. They are easier to prepare than runner beans, as they simply need to be "topped and tailed".

Available: All year round.

Storage: In a cool place.

Preparation: All you need to do is to trim off the stalk and the pointed end where the flower once was. You can cut the beans into even lengths of about 2.5cm (1 inch), but if they are not too big to fit in your saucepan, they can be left whole.

Cooking: Cook in boiling salted water for 10–15 minutes. Drain and serve.

Other uses: French beans are delicious lightly cooked, chilled and added to salads, such as salade niçoise. They also work well in a vegetable curry, adding some crunch if not overcooked.

Runner beans

Available: July to October.
Storage: In a cool place.
Preparation: Unless they are a special variety, you need to "string" runner beans. This means running a sharp knife all round the outside edge of the bean, taking off a thin layer. You will find that one edge of the bean has a thin ridge that is easy to trim, while the other side is flatter. Include the top and bottom of the bean as you trim to remove the stalk and the remains of the flower. Slice into diagonal pieces, about 5mm (1/4 inch) wide. If the bean puts up a bit of a fight as you cut, it may be old and tough, so discard it. One tough bean in a serving can spoil the whole lot.
Cooking: Cook in boiling salted water for 12–15 minutes. Drain and serve.
Other uses: Left-over cooked beans make a tasty, if not too nutritionally sound, snack if fried in hot oil with diced cooked potatoes.

Broccoli

This may be the purple or white type, traditionally grown in this country, where a small flower nestles among dark leaves, or calabrese, which has much larger heads and a thick green stalk, looking like a small, dark-green cauliflower.
Available: All year round (calabrese), February to May (purple and white).
Storage: Keep in a cool, dark place.
Preparation: Trim the excess, tough stalk off purple or white broccoli, losing only a few of the leaves, and wash thoroughly. For calabrese, trim the florets off the head and discard the thickest part of the stalk.
Cooking: Cook either type in boiling salted water for 10–12 minutes, until just tender. Drain and serve.

Brussels sprouts

These have come to be known as a traditional part of Christmas lunch and a nightmare to some small children, but a well cooked sprout can be delicious.

Available: September to April.

Storage: Keep cool. If they are still on the stalk, they will keep longer than if they have already been trimmed off.

Preparation: Trim away a small part of the stalk and remove any outside leaves that this loosens or that look a bit tired. If the sprout is large, cut a cross into the base of the stalk, as this will help it to cook more evenly.

Cooking: Cook in boiling salted water for 12–15 minutes until just tender when stabbed with a sharp knife. Over-cooking is what produces the brussels sprout from hell!

Other uses: Left-over cooked sprouts mashed with left-over cooked potatoes make excellent bubble and squeak (page 89).

Cabbage

There are so many varieties of cabbage available, from dark green and pointed ones, to pale green, round and hard ones, crinkly savoys and colourful red cabbages.

Available: All year round.

Storage: Kept in a cool, dark place, they will remain fresh for several weeks.

Preparation: Cut the cabbage into quarters through the stalk, then trim away the white, woody part of the stalk. Shred the remaining cabbage into slices about 5mm (1/4 inch) wide.

Cooking: Cook the shredded cabbage in boiling salted water for 10–12 minutes. Drain and serve. Red cabbage is delicious casseroled (see page 129).

Other uses: White cabbage is an essential ingredient in traditional coleslaw (page 131) and is also good, finely shredded, in stir-fries.

Carrots

With their bright orange, juicy flesh, carrots look absolutely bursting with health. They are particularly good eaten raw.

Available: All year round. Baby carrots from June to August.

Storage: In a cool, dry place.

Preparation: Baby carrots simply need to be trimmed top and bottom to remove the leaves and excess root and thoroughly washed. You *can* scrape them to remove the skin, but this is not necessary. Old carrots should be peeled (a potato-peeler is the best tool for this), trimmed and cut into 5mm (1/4 inch) slices, or you can cut them lengthways into thin chips.

Cooking: Baby carrots: cook in boiling salted water for 10–12 minutes. Drain and serve. Old carrots: place in a pan, cover with cold water and add salt. Bring to the boil and simmer for 15–20 minutes.

Other uses: Uncooked carrots are another ingredient in coleslaw (page 131). Carrots add colour and flavour to stews and casseroles.

Cauliflower

This provides an excellent foil for green vegetables and offers a different shape and texture.

Available: All year round, but at their best between June and October.

Storage: In a cool place.

Preparation: Cauliflowers usually arrive in a nest of leaves. Cut through the base, just where the florets start, and discard the leaves and the tough base of the stalk. Trim into individual florets, away from the stalk.

Cooking: Cook in boiling salted water for 10–12 minutes, until just tender when pierced with a sharp knife.

Other uses: Delicious with cheese sauce (page 91), cauliflower is also excellent in a vegetable curry – its texture seems to absorb the flavours very well.

Celery

Where I live, market stalls are piled high in the autumn with Fenland celery, the roots still black with the rich soil. The smell is amazing and reminds one that this is much more than a watery salad vegetable.

Available: All year round.

Storage: Keep in the refrigerator.

Preparation: Cut through the bunch about 2.5cm (1 inch) from the base, which will free the outer stalks, then cut into quarters through the root and cut each piece into half again. Wash well.

Cooking: Celery can be cooked in boiling salted water for 20 minutes, but is particularly good braised. Arrange the prepared celery in an ovenproof dish, add 150ml (5 fl oz) of water or stock, dot with butter and cover. Cook in an oven preheated to 180°C/350°F/Gas Mark 4 for about 1½ hours, until tender.

Other uses: Celery is delicious raw and makes a good accompaniment to a cheese board. It is great sliced in stews and has an excellent flavour in soups.

Courgettes

These have become much more common in recent years and are so quick and easy to prepare and cook. Choose small, evenly sized courgettes for the best flavour and cooking results.

Available: All year round.

Storage: Keep in the refrigerator.

Preparation: Do not peel. Trim off both ends and then cut into 5mm (¹/₄ inch) slices. Very small courgettes can be left whole.

Cooking: Place in a pan, add about 60ml (4tbspn) of water and a pinch of salt, cover tightly and cook over a high heat for 8–10 minutes, gently shaking the pan occasionally. Drain and serve. Alternatively, heat 45ml (3tbspn) of oil in a pan over a medium to high heat and fry the courgette slices for 2–3 minutes on each side.

Other uses: Courgettes can be stuffed by cutting in half lengthways, hollowing out the middle like mini canoes and filling with a stuffing of your choice before baking until tender. They are an essential ingredient in ratatouille (page 133).

Cucumber

Either as a salad vegetable or lightly sautéed, cucumber has a delicate flavour. Cucumbers are sold whole, in halves, or portioned, so choose the size that suits you best.

Available: All year round, though prices do fluctuate.

Storage: Keep in the refrigerator.

Preparation: If serving cucumber in a salad, remove strips of the skin, using a potato-peeler, and then cut into thin slices. If cooking, peel completely and cut into cubes about 1cm (¹/₂ inch) in each direction.

Cooking: Melt 25g (1oz) of butter in a pan over a medium heat. Add the cucumber and cook, turning occasionally, for about 10 minutes.

Other uses: Cucumber makes a delicious chilled soup. Peel, dice and cook in stock until tender. Purée, season and chill. Stir in double cream before serving. Don't forget the cucumber sandwich, a teatime treat.

Leeks

Choose leeks that have a long white stalk and fresh green leaves. Select vegetables of similar sizes for even cooking.

Available: August to May.

Storage: Keep in a cool, dry place.

Preparation: The big trick with leeks is to remove the grit that always seems to become embedded between the layers of leaves. First trim the root and leaves and peel off any damaged layers. Then split the leek down the middle and rinse thoroughly. This method is efficient but spoils the shape of the leek as it does tend to fall apart when cooking. My method is to trim the leek as above and then cut it into 1cm (1/2 inch) slices, starting from the root end. The dirt tends to be at the leaf end, so as soon as any grit appears in your slices, toss them into a sieve and swoosh under a fast-running cold tap.

Cooking: Place in a pan, cover with cold water and add 2.5ml (1/2tspn) of salt. Cover, bring to the boil and simmer for 15–20 minutes. You can also cook leeks in an oven. Cut in half lengthways and place in an ovenproof dish with 30ml (2tbspn) of water, 25g (1oz) of butter and a pinch of salt and pepper. Cover and bake in an oven preheated to 180°C/350°F/Gas Mark 4 for about 1 hour, or until tender when pierced with a sharp knife.Cooking times are a bit less critical with this method, and you can keep the leeks warm quite happily if the rest of the meal isn't ready.

Other uses: Leeks make the base of a great soup (page 78). They are also delicious cooked whole, wrapped in slices of ham and smothered in cheese sauce.

Lettuce

There is now a frightening range of lettuces available: soft, crispy, green, red, flat, curly and so forth. The secret is to find the type you prefer or which best suits your application. It is worthwhile considering the bags of prepared mixed lettuce that are now widely available. They may seem expensive but, unless you are catering for a football team, it is a way of getting a range of flavours and textures without filling your fridge with half-eaten lettuces.

Available: All year round.

Storage: In a refrigerator.

Preparation: Different lettuces require different handling. In all cases, trim the stalk and discard any tired-looking outside leaves. Soft, open lettuces can simply have the leaves pulled away from the stalk. Crisper, tighter varieties are best dealt with a bit like a cabbage. Cut into quarters through the stalk and shred across as finely as you wish.

Marrow

This is a true love-it or hate-it vegetable. Buy small marrows that do not sound too hollow when you tap them gently.

Available: June to October.

Storage: In a cool place.

Preparation: Cut across into slices about 2.5cm (1 inch) thick, discarding the ends. Peel away the skin and push out the seeds and fuzzy white membrane in the centre. Leave as rings or cut into chunks.

Cooking: Boil in salted water for 10 minutes. Drain very thoroughly.

Other uses: Marrow is another vegetable that is delicious smothered in cheese sauce. It is also excellent stuffed and baked (see page 132).

Mushrooms

Once again shops and supermarkets now offer us a much wider choice of mushrooms than ever before. As well as the standard white type, available as buttons, open caps and flat mushrooms, you will also find chestnut mushrooms, which have a firmer texture and slightly stronger flavour. A variety of exotic oriental mushrooms, such as shitake, are joined in the autumn by some exciting continental varieties, such as chanterelles and ceps (porcini). These quite often have cooking and serving suggestions on the packets.

Available: Standard: all year round; others by season.

Storage: Keep in a refrigerator, but not in a tightly sealed plastic bag as they will sweat and spoil.

Preparation: If mushrooms are cultivated, they do not have to be peeled, unless you prefer them so. Just wipe them with a piece of kitchen paper and trim the end off the stalk.

Cooking: Cut into thick slices and fry in a little oil or butter over a medium heat for 10 minutes, turning occasionally. Or leave whole and grill, stalk side up, with a small piece of butter on each one, under a medium heat, for 10 minutes.

Onions

For most of the recipes in this book, ordinary cooking onions are ideal, but if you want to include raw sliced onions in a dish such as a salad, try red onions, which look most attractive.

Available: All year round.

Storage: Keep in a cool, dark place.

Preparation: Trim the top and bottom and peel off the outer skin. Cut into thin slices or chop. The best way to chop an onion is to cut it in half from top to stalk. Lay the cut side down on a chopping board, and cut vertical slices through the top, holding the onion together with your fingers (but being careful to keep them away from the knife). Now cut down into slices again across the onion. The thickness of slices will determine whether your pieces are chopped finely or coarsely. This process sounds complicated but is actually quite easy and when you have done it a few times you'll be surprised at how professional you look.

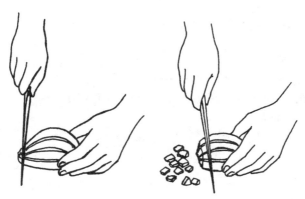

Cooking: Onions, with their cooking instructions, are included in many of the savoury recipes in this book. They are also delicious baked. Leave the onions whole but wash and trim the root. Place in a shallow, ovenproof dish and bake in an oven preheated to 200°C/400°F/Gas Mark 6 for 1–1$1/4$ hours for a medium-sized onion. Pierce with a sharp knife to check that the onion is soft.

Parsnips

This root vegetable is often ignored, which is a shame. Its lovely, slightly sweet flavour is particularly good when roasted.

Available: September to April.

Storage: In a cool, dark place.

Preparation: Choose smallish parsnips that are stubby rather than long and thin. Larger vegetables run the risk of having a woody centre. Trim the top and root and peel quite thickly with a sharp knife or potato-peeler. Cut into evenly sized pieces. I find the best way to do this is to cut the parsnip in half across the middle, then cut the top piece lengthways into four chunks and cut the bottom piece into two or leave it whole if thin.

Cooking: Roast parsnips: cut as above and place in a pan of boiling salted water. Simmer for 5 minutes, then drain. Heat 45–60ml (4–5tbspn) of vegetable oil in a roasting tin for 10 minutes, in an oven preheated to 200°C/400°F/Gas Mark 6. Remove from the oven and quickly but carefully add the blanched parsnip pieces and turn each with a fork to ensure that they are evenly covered with oil. Return to the oven and roast for 45–50 minutes until dark golden around the edges and soft when pierced with a sharp knife. Peeled parsnips can also be cut into chip-sized pieces and cooked in boiling salted water for 20–25 minutes.

Other uses: Chunks of parsnip can be added to stews and casseroles and grated parsnip can be used in cakes instead of grated carrot.

Peas

Fresh young peas, straight from the pod, are a summertime treat. At other times, well cooked frozen peas are a perfectly acceptable alternative.

Available: June to September (frozen: all year round).

Storage: In a cool, dry place.

Preparation: To shell peas, press on the seam at the pointed end, not the stalk end. The pod should pop open so you can unzip it and scoop out the peas. Remember that a large pile of peas in their pods can produce a fairly disappointing amount of shelled peas, so be generous when buying.

Cooking: Cook in boiling salted water for 10 minutes. Drain and serve, topped with a chunk of butter.

Potatoes

Surely one of the most versatile of all vegetables, potatoes are now a vital ingredient of cookery around the world. Chipped, roast, baked, mashed, boiled, sautéed and included in a whole range of classic dishes, the potato is a staple part of the British diet. If you buy your potatoes in supermarkets, you will find the bags advise you on the best cooking methods for that particular variety. Try to find one that is general purpose, as it is not practical to store five different varieties for five different cooking methods. The only variety I would specifically mention is King Edward, in my opinion the only potato for roasting.

Available: All year round.

Storage: In a cool, dark place.

Preparation: Potatoes for baking in their jackets should simply be washed and dried. For other methods of cooking, they should be thinly peeled, either with a potato-peeler or with a small, sharp knife.

Cooking: There are numerous ways of cooking potatoes. I have described a few favourites below.

Boiling and mashing: Peel the potatoes and cut into even-sized chunks. Place in a pan with 2.5ml (1/2tspn) of salt and cover with cold water and a lid. Place on the hob on a high heat and bring to the boil, then reduce the heat and simmer for about 20 minutes, or until the potatoes feel tender when pierced with a sharp knife. Drain and serve. For mashed potatoes, proceed as above. Once drained, attack the potatoes with a masher or fork and reduce to a smooth paste. Then add about 25g (1oz) of butter, a good pinch of black pepper and enough milk to make a creamy mash. Beat with a wooden spoon until light and fluffy.

Roasting: Proceed as for boiled potatoes but when the water comes to the boil, turn off the heat and leave the potatoes in the water for 5 minutes. Drain. Then place the lid back on the pan, hold on to it and shake the pan quite vigorously. This will make the edges break up and result in wonderfully crispy potatoes. Meanwhile, heat about 5mm (¼ inch) of vegetable oil in a roasting tin in an oven preheated to 200°C/400°F/Gas Mark 6 for 10 minutes. Remove the pan from the oven and quickly but carefully add the potatoes. With the help of a fork, turn them around in the oil so that they are evenly coated. Quickly return the pan to the oven and cook for 1¼–1½ hours, turning them over halfway through the cooking time, until the potatoes are crisp and golden but tender in the centre when pierced with a fork.

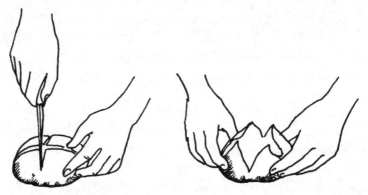

Baking: Try to choose evenly sized potatoes weighing about 225–275g (8–10oz) each. It is important to slit or prick the potatoes before baking or there is a danger that they will burst when they are in the oven. Either cut a shallow slit all around the middle of the potato, or cut a deep cross in the top. If you are planning to stuff the potatoes and therefore need to slice them in half, a cut around the middle is best. You can also prick the potatoes all over with a fork. Then place them on a baking tray or directly on the oven shelf in an oven preheated to 200°C/400°F/Gas Mark 6 for 1^1/4–1^1/2 hours, until the outside is crispy and the middle is soft when prodded with a knife. Baked potatoes are remarkably well behaved, so if necessary you can cook them longer at a lower temperature. To present baked potatoes attractively, prepare with a crisscross slit in the top. When cooked, squeeze the potato either side of the slit and it should crack open and puff up, inviting a large knob of butter to be placed on top.

Cold cooked potatoes: These are a gift to any cook. Cooked, whole potatoes can be cut into slices about 5mm (^{1}/4 inch) thick and fried in a little vegetable oil over a medium to high heat for 3–4 minutes on each side, to give crisp and golden sauté potatoes. Cold mashed potatoes can be combined with any other leftover vegetables and fried to give bubble and squeak (page 89), or they can be made into potato cake (page 227). Any kind of mashed or sliced cooked potato can also be used as a topping, for example on cottage pie, fish pie or on a vegetable casserole.

Swedes

Choose smallish swedes, about the size of two fists put together, as they can become tough and woody as they get larger.

Available: September to June.

Storage: In a cool, dark place.

Preparation: Peel swedes quite thickly. You may find them easier to peel if you first cut them in half from leaf end to root. Then cut into chunks about 3cm (1^1/4 inch) square. Swedes can put up a bit of a fight, so choose a sharp and heavy cook's knife and keep your fingers clear.

Cooking: Place in a pan and cover with cold water. Add 2.5ml (^{1}/2tspn) of salt, cover and bring to the boil. Simmer for about 20 minutes, until tender when pierced with a sharp knife. Drain and serve.

Other uses: Swede is delicious cooked as above and mashed with a lump of butter and lots of black pepper. A pinch of ground nutmeg adds an interesting flavour. You can also mash swedes with equal quantities of potatoes or carrots, which can be cut into chunks and cooked with the swede. Diced swede can be added to stews and casseroles.

Sweet peppers

Once just available as green or red, you can now also buy yellow and orange peppers. They are lovely cut up and used in salads, where they add flavour and colour.

Available: All year round.

Storage: Keep in a refrigerator.

Preparation: Cut in half from stalk to tip and scoop out the little white seeds. A quick wash under the cold tap will dislodge any hiding in crevices. I also like to cut away the three or four thick membranes, as they spoil the shape of your slice or dice. For adding to casseroles or salads, cut into strips or squares to a size that suits the dish you are preparing.

Cooking: Generally, peppers are only cooked if they are part of a dish such as ratatouille (page 133), and they are also delicious stuffed. Cut in half and deseed as above. Place halves, open side up, in a lightly oiled ovenproof dish and fill with the stuffing of your choice. The one used for stuffed marrow (page 132) would work well, or you could make a vegetarian version using bread-crumbs, diced onion, crushed garlic, chopped mushrooms, sweet-corn kernels and chopped celery, or any other vegetable combination you have to hand. Cover the dish with a lid or foil and bake in an oven preheated to 200°C/400°F/Gas Mark 6 for 30–40 minutes, until the peppers are soft. Any colour of pepper can be used for this, or you could use a combination – traffic-light stuffed peppers!

Tomatoes

Technically a fruit, tomatoes are, in most people's eyes, a most versatile vegetable. You will now find standard, plum, cherry and beefsteak tomatoes in stores. In most recipes, standard tomatoes are fine, though cherry tomatoes look attractive in a salad.

Available: All year round.

Storage: In a refrigerator.

Preparation: Apart from removing the calyx (green star-shaped part at the top), your tomato is basically ready for action. Some recipes will expect you to skin tomatoes and this is very easily achieved. Place the tomatoes in a bowl and cover with boiling water. Leave for two minutes. During this time, I like to viciously stab each tomato a couple of times with a small, sharp knife. This causes the skin to split, which makes peeling easier. Then, tip off the boiling water and replace with cold. Finally, simply squidge the tomatoes between your fingers and you should find the skin slips off quite easily. Don't turn your back on the tomatoes while they are in the boiling water. If you leave them too long, the flesh starts to cook and skinning becomes rather messy.

Cooking: Grilled or baked tomatoes make a great accompaniment to chops or sausages. To grill, cut in half through the stalk, place cut side up on a grill rack and sprinkle with a pinch of salt and pepper. Cook under a medium grill for about 10 minutes until browning on top and slightly puffed up. To bake, leave whole and place in a shallow ovenproof dish, stalk end down (they balance better that way). Then, cut a cross in each top and squeeze a small piece of butter into it. Sprinkle each tomato with a pinch of salt and pepper and place, uncovered, in an oven preheated to 200°C/400°F/Gas Mark 6 for about 20 minutes. The skin around the cross should start to char and peel back a bit, which looks most attractive.

Other uses: Stuffed tomatoes are simple to prepare. Place tomatoes stalk end down and cut off a lid from the top (about 1/8 of the tomato). Scoop out the seeds using a small spoon and taking care not to damage the shell. Fill with a stuffing of your choice (see sweet peppers) and top with the lid, set at a jaunty angle. Place on a shallow ovenproof dish and bake, uncovered, in an oven preheated to 180°C/350°F/Gas Mark 4 for 25–30 minutes. For hearty appetites, use beefsteak tomatoes and bake for 40–45 minutes.

Turnips

Although large turnips are available, I would choose the baby ones, no bigger than a small apple and a beautiful white and mauve colour.

Available: All year round.

Storage: In a cool, dark place.

Preparation: Peel the turnips quite thickly and cut into chunks about 2.5cm (1 inch) square.

Cooking: Place in a pan, cover with cold water and add 2.5ml (1/2tspn) of salt. Bring to the boil and simmer for about 20 minutes, until tender when pierced with a fork. Drain and serve.

Other uses: Parsnips are another vegetable that is great in stews and casseroles.

SAGE DERBY LAYER

This is such a delicious vegetable recipe that it makes an excellent supper, perhaps served with salad, or you could serve smaller portions with cold meats or sausages.

Preparation time: 30 minutes
Cooking time: 1½ hours

You will need:
175g (6oz) Sage Derby cheese, grated
700g (1½lb) potatoes, peeled and thinly sliced
225g (8oz) onions, peeled and thinly sliced
75g (3oz) butter or margarine, cut into small pieces
Salt and pepper

1 Smear a 1–1½ litre (1¾–2½ pint) ovenproof dish with a little of the butter.

2 Cover the base of the dish with about a third of the potato slices, spread out evenly.

3 Add half the onion slices and sprinkle with half the cheese. Add a pinch of salt and pepper and about a third of the butter.

4 Repeat these layers, leaving about 30ml (2tbspn) of the cheese to one side, and then cover with the remaining potato slices. If you like, you can arrange these in overlapping circles.

5 Arrange the remaining butter over the surface of the potatoes and sprinkle with the cheese you have saved.

6 Place in an oven preheated to 180°C/350°F/Gas Mark 4 and cook for about 1½ hours. Push a sharp knife deep into the potatoes – they should feel soft and not crispy. If they do not feel cooked, return the casserole to the oven for a further 20 minutes and retest.

Cook's Tip

Sage Derby is a hard yellow cheese, marbled with green streaks of sage. If you cannot find it, make the dish with cheddar, adding a sprinkling of dried sage to each onion layer. You could also experiment with other cheeses and flavourings.

POTATOES O'BRIEN

Potatoes cooked this way become the star of any meal. A supper dish in its own right, this recipe makes an excellent accompaniment to grilled meats or casseroles.

Preparation time: 25 minutes
Cooking time: 1 hour

You will need:

1kg (2.2lb) potatoes, peeled
1 large green pepper, deseeded and
    finely chopped
1 large onion, finely chopped
15ml (1tbspn) plain flour
45ml (3tbspn) chopped parsley

110g (4oz) cheddar cheese, grated
Pinch salt and pepper
25g (1oz) butter
150ml (5 fl oz) milk
150ml (5 fl oz) double cream

1 Cut the potatoes into slices about 5mm (^{1}/4 inch) thick. Then cut each slice into strips about 5mm (^{1}/4 inch) wide and then cut across into squares, which should give you neat little cubes. Place these in a large bowl with the chopped pepper and onion and mix together well.

2 Sprinkle in the flour, parsley, cheese, salt and pepper and mix thoroughly. (Hands are the best tools for this job.)

3 Smear a little of the butter around the base and sides of a large ovenproof dish. Turn the potato mixture into the dish and spread out evenly.

4 Heat the milk and cream together in a pan over a high heat until just beginning to bubble, pour over the potatoes and dot with the butter. Do not cover.

5 Place in an oven preheated to 190°C/375°F/Gas Mark 5 for about 1 hour. The surface should be crisp and the potatoes feel soft when prodded with a knife.

BRAISED RED CABBAGE

However small a red cabbage you buy, you will discover that it is densely packed and produces an awful lot of vegetable when shredded. This recipe keeps well and can be gently reheated with no problems but also freezes most successfully.

Preparation time: 30 minutes
Cooking time: 2¹/₂ hours

You will need:

About 1kg (2.2lb) red cabbage

450g (1lb) onions

450g (1lb) cooking apples

5ml (1tspn) mixed spice

45ml (3tbspn) soft brown sugar

Salt and pepper

45ml (3tbspn) red wine or cider vinegar

1 First deal with the cabbage. Peel off any tired-looking outer leaves, then cut the cabbage into halves and quarters through the stalk. This is actually easier said than done – red cabbages are pretty solid and your knife tends to get stuck halfway through. Just keep attacking it from all sides with a very sharp knife and a lot of care until it finally submits. Then cut away the white stalky part and shred the cabbage into fine slices.

2 Peel and finely slice the onions and peel and chop the apples. Now begin assembling. Take a large casserole and add about a third of the cabbage, sprinkle with about half of the onions and apples, then sprinkle with half the spice and sugar and some salt and pepper. Repeat these layers and finish with the final third of the cabbage, which will probably now be bursting out of the dish. Press it down well, as it will cook down. Pour the vinegar over and cover with a tightly fitting lid or a double layer of foil.

3 Now place the prepared casserole in an oven preheated to 150°C/300°F/Gas Mark 2 for about 2 1/2 hours, giving it a quick stir after about 1 hour. By the end of the cooking time, the cabbage should be quite tender.

This is delicious served with cold meats or casseroles and baked potatoes.

COLESLAW

When one buys this ready-made, it is in small tubs and one feels obliged to eat small portions. I like to make large bowlfuls and eat large amounts! Remember it is also delicious in a sandwich or spooned into a baked potato and, being more robust than a green salad, will keep, covered, in a refrigerator for several days. Bearing in mind the large raw onion content, it is probably worth making sure anyone close to you shares this treat!

Preparation time: 30 minutes

You will need:
1 small, hard, white cabbage – about 450–700g (1–1¹/₂lb)
2 onions
4 large carrots
About 275ml (10 fl oz) good quality mayonnaise

1 Cut the cabbage into quarters through the stem and trim away the hard white stalk, any thick leaf veins and any damaged outside leaves.

2 Now cut across and shred the cabbage into very fine strips. Place in a large mixing bowl.

3 Peel the onions, cut into quarters and cut across into very fine slices. Add to the cabbage in the bowl.

4 Peel the carrots and grate on the coarsest side of your grater. Add to the cabbage and onion and mix well to combine.

5 Now pour in the mayonnaise – you can add a bit less or more depending on personal taste – and mix well. Pile into a serving bowl (or leave in the mixing bowl if you believe in economy of washing up!) and chill before serving.

STUFFED MARROW

If you find marrow a little bland, and I suspect only a dedicated marrow-eater wouldn't, then try this recipe.

Preparation time: 25 minutes
Cooking time: 35 minutes

You will need:

1 medium marrow
30ml (2tbspn) vegetable oil
1 large onion, peeled and chopped
1 clove garlic, crushed
2 stalks celery, chopped
350g (12oz) mince – beef, pork, turkey
    or meat substitute

110g (4oz) mushrooms, chopped
110g (4oz) fresh white breadcrumbs
Small can sweetcorn kernels, drained
Pinch dried mixed herbs
Salt and pepper

1 Heat the oil in a pan over a medium heat. Add the onion, garlic and celery and cook for 5 minutes, until beginning to soften and brown.

2 Remove from the heat and add the mince, mushrooms, breadcrumbs, sweetcorn, herbs and a pinch of salt and pepper.

3 Cut the marrow into slices about 2.5cm (1 inch) thick. Peel and push out the seeds, trimming away any stringy bits with a sharp knife. Ideally, you should end up with eight rings.

4 Place the rings on an oiled roasting tin (you may have to use two) and divide the stuffing between them, pushing it gently to fill the holes. Any excess can just be piled on top.

5 Cook, uncovered, in an oven preheated to 200°C/400°F/Gas Mark 6 for about 30–35 minutes, until the marrow feels tender when pierced with a sharp knife. Remove the tray from the oven carefully, as quite a lot of free liquid can accumulate during cooking.

RATATOUILLE

This Mediterranean vegetable dish can be served hot or cold as a starter, an accompaniment to grilled meat, or with crusty bread as a light vegetarian meal.

Preparation time: 40 minutes
Cooking time: 1½ hours

You will need:

1 medium aubergine
Salt
75ml (5tbspn) vegetable oil
450g (1lb) tomatoes
1 green pepper

1 red pepper
450g (1lb) courgettes
2 large onions
1 clove garlic
Pinch salt and pepper

1 First prepare the vegetables. Do not peel the aubergine but cut it into slices about 5mm (¼ inch) thick. Spread out on a tray and sprinkle with salt. Leave for 20 minutes, then rinse, drain and pat dry with kitchen paper. This draws out the excess moisture. If you don't have time to do this, it is not the end of the world, but your finished dish will just be a bit more sloppy. Peel the tomatoes (see page 125) and cut them into quarters. Halve the peppers, remove the seeds and cut into strips. Trim the ends off the courgettes and cut into 5mm (¼ inch) slices. Peel and chop the onions and crush the garlic.

2 Now heat the oil in a pan over a medium to high heat. Add as many aubergine slices as will fit and fry for 2–3 minutes on each side. Remove from the pan and repeat with the remaining slices.

3 When these have all been fried and removed, add the remaining ingredients to the pan and cook, stirring, for 5 minutes.

4 Turn the mixture into a large casserole dish, add the aubergine slices and mix well.

5 Cover and cook in an oven preheated to 180°C/350°F/Gas Mark 4 for about 1½ hours until the vegetables are soft.

Cook's Tip

You can use a tin of chopped tomatoes in juice instead of the fresh ones. If you have any, a little olive oil drizzled over the finished dish is delicious.

MAIN
DISHES

RECIPES

CHICKEN STIR-FRY

Tender pieces of chicken breast and a variety of vegetables are quickly cooked with a Chinese-style sauce.

SAUSAGE AND BEAN CASSEROLE

A quick-to-cook dish that is warming and hearty – ideal for bonfire night.

STEAK UPSIDE-DOWN PIE

An unusual dish – savoury mince under a cheesy scone crust.

MEATLOAF

Mince can be made to go a long way in this savoury supper dish that is likely to become a firm favourite.

CORNED BEEF HASH

Corned beef, potatoes and onions, fried together and warmed with Worcestershire sauce, make a wonderfully comforting winter dish.

SAVOURY BATTER

A simple batter recipe, which is easily extended to make toad-in-the-hole and Yorkshire pudding.

PASTA AND SAUCES

Try any of the huge variety of pastas now available with the sauces suggested here.

RISOTTO

A savoury rice dish, flavoured with tomatoes and mushrooms, that can be adapted in a variety of ways.

LEEK AND BEAN PAN-FRY

A quick supper dish, with all the ingredients cooked together in one pan.

ITALIAN LIVER

If you have disliked liver since you were a child, do try this recipe – you might just become a convert!

BEEF AND ONION PATTIES

Savoury cakes, made of corned beef, mashed potato and seasoning, are quickly flash-fried to make a delicious supper dish.

FRANKFURTER AND BEAN HOTPOT

Another one-pan dish, quick to cook and full of flavoursome ingredients.

SAUSAGE SIZZLE

Use a can of condensed soup to make this quick and easy sausage dish.

BEEF STEW AND DUMPLINGS

A classic recipe that can be varied to create beef in beer and chicken casserole.

SAVOURY MINCE

Master this basic recipe and see how easy it is to make spaghetti bolognese, cottage pie or chilli con carne.

VEGETABLE COBBLER

A mixture of vegetables, unusually flavoured with orange juice, and topped with cheese scones.

CHEESE PUDDING

Milk, eggs, cheese and breadcrumbs all combine to make a light and fluffy pudding.

VEGETABLE CURRY

Use this basic recipe as the starting point for all sorts of curry dishes.

HADDOCK IN CIDER

An elegant dish, haddock poached with celery and cider is delicious with rice or pasta.

TUNA OR SALMON FISHCAKES

Fish and mashed potatoes are mixed and shaped into little cakes to be crisply fried.

PRAWN AND RICE SALAD

A lovely light dish, which combines cooked rice with prawns, chicken, mushrooms and apples in a piquant dressing.

FISH PIE

An extra quick and easy way to make this classic dish.

TUNA FISH PIE

Tuna fish, baked beans and mashed potatoes sound an odd combination, but they go together remarkably well in this delicious supper dish.

CHICKEN STIR-FRY

Stir-frying is a quick and nutritious way of cooking. It also has the happy ability to make a little meat go a long way. You certainly do not need a wok to stir-fry – a large frying pan is perfectly adequate – and don't be afraid to get it steaming hot, as this is the secret of a good stir-fry. The vegetable choice in this recipe is just a suggestion, as you can use whatever you like.

Preparation time: 20 minutes
Cooking time: 15 minutes

You will need:

2 large chicken breast fillets, without skin
1 large onion
1 clove garlic
2 large carrots
1 small green pepper
1 small packet mange-tout peas
A small bunch of spring onions
110g (4oz) button mushrooms

1 small leek
30ml (2tbspn) vegetable oil
110g (4oz) beansprouts
25g (1oz) unsalted peanuts or cashews
10ml (2tspn) cornflour
30ml (2tbspn) soy sauce
30ml (2tbspn) sherry

1 Cut the chicken into thin strips across the diagonal of the meat.

2 Peel the onion, cut it in half and slice thinly. Finely chop the garlic. Peel the carrots and cut into pieces the size of matchsticks. Deseed the pepper and cut into thin strips. Top and tail

the mange-tout. Trim the roots and leaves of the spring onions and cut into 2.5cm (1 inch) slices. Slice the mushrooms. Wash the leek thoroughly and cut into thin slices.

3 Place the oil in a large frying pan over a high heat and wait until it just starts to smoke. Quickly add the chicken and cook for 2 minutes, turning it around the pan with a wooden spoon.

4 Add the onion, garlic, carrot, pepper, mange-tout, spring onions, mushrooms and leek and toss around the pan with a wooden spoon until they just begin to soften (about 5–7 minutes). Test that the chicken is cooked by breaking a piece in half – it should break easily and be opaque right through.

5 Add the beansprouts and nuts and mix around in the pan for 1 minute, until heated through.

6 Quickly mix together the cornflour, soy sauce and sherry in a small bowl or cup and pour rapidly over the vegetable mixture, stirring all the time. If you don't stir vigorously, the glaze will all congeal in one spot. If you would like a little more sauce, stir in 30ml (2tbspn) water.

7 Serve at once with rice or noodles.

SAUSAGE AND BEAN CASSEROLE

This is a hearty but very quickly prepared casserole, guaranteed to take the chill off the coldest night. Serve with crusty bread or baked potatoes.

Preparation time: 20 minutes
Cooking time: 30 minutes

You will need:

15ml (1tbspn) vegetable oil

1 large onion, chopped

2 sticks of celery, cut into 5mm (1/4 inch) slices

1 clove of garlic, crushed

Pinch of chilli powder

450g (1lb) spicy sausage – the cooked type found on delicatessen counters

400g (14oz) can chopped tomatoes in juice

15ml (1tbspn) tomato purée

30ml (2tbspn) Worcestershire sauce

150ml (5 fl oz) water

400g (14oz) can mixed beans, drained

400g (14oz) can baked beans

1 Heat the oil in the pan over a medium heat. Add the onion, celery and garlic and cook, stirring, for 5 minutes. Add the chilli powder and cook for a further minute.

2 Cut the sausage into thick slices and add to the onion mixture with the tomatoes, purée, Worcestershire sauce and water. Stir well and heat until just beginning to bubble.

3 Remove from the heat, stir in both types of beans, and transfer to an ovenproof dish with a lid. If you have a casserole dish that can be used on the hob and in the oven, you can use this for both operations and save on the washing up.

4 Place in an oven preheated to 200°C/400°F/Gas Mark 6 for 30 minutes.

STEAK UPSIDE-DOWN PIE

This is an unusual dish that allows a small amount of mince to serve 4 people.

Preparation time: 35 minutes
Cooking time: 50 minutes

You will need:

MEAT LAYER

30ml (2tbspn) vegetable oil
2 onions, peeled and chopped
110g (4oz) mushrooms, sliced
3 tomatoes, peeled and chopped finely
1 beef stock cube
275ml (10 fl oz) water
350g (12oz) minced beef

TOPPING

175g (6oz) self-raising flour
Salt and pepper
2.5ml ($1/2$tspn) mustard powder
50g (2oz) soft margarine
50g (2oz) cheddar cheese, grated
1 egg yolk
Milk

1 Heat the vegetable oil in a large pan over a medium heat and add the onions, mushrooms and tomatoes. Fry, stirring gently with a wooden spoon, for 5 minutes.

2 Add the water and stock cube and stir to dissolve. Add the meat, stirring to break up the lumps, and cook for 15 minutes, stirring occasionally. The mix should be quite thick by this time. Pour it into a 17.5–20cm (7–8 inch) round ovenproof dish, about 10cm (4 inches) deep. Allow to cool slightly while you make the topping.

3 Sieve the flour, a pinch of salt and pepper, and the mustard powder into a large bowl. Add the margarine and rub between your fingers until the fat is mixed into the flour and there are no big lumps left.

4 Stir in the cheese and mix in the egg yolk. Now add enough milk to make a soft dough. The best way to do this is to use your fingers and add the milk a little at a time until the mixture begins to form a ball. Knead gently to make a larger ball, adding a bit more milk if you can't pick up all the flour. Don't worry, this will all make sense as you actually make the topping.

5 Roll out the dough on a floured work-surface into a round to fit the top of your dish. Don't worry if the edges are a bit ragged, as they won't show in the finished dish. Lay the round gently on top of the mince mixture, pushing down the edges to fit over the meat.

6 Place in an oven preheated to 180°C/350°F/Gas Mark 4 for 45–50 minutes, until the top is crisp and golden.

7 Turn out on to a plate, so the crust is at the bottom with the mince on top, and serve. Mashed potatoes and cabbage go well with this dish.

MEATLOAF

Ideally, this dish should be cooked in a loaf tin, but it will taste fine baked in a round casserole if necessary – simply cut into wedges instead of slices when you serve it. This is a fairly basic recipe and very easily prepared, but it makes a good lunch or supper dish served with baked potatoes and vegetables or salad.

Preparation time: 15 minutes
Cooking time: 1¹/₄hours

You will need:

450g (1lb) beef mince
110g (4oz) mushrooms, finely chopped
1 large onion, finely chopped
1 clove garlic, crushed
45ml (3tbspn) tomato purée

50g (2oz) fresh white breadcrumbs
Pinch of salt and pepper
15ml (1tbspn) Worcestershire sauce
1 egg, beaten

1 In a large bowl, mix together all the ingredients until very well blended.

2 Grease a 1kg (2lb) loaf tin or other similarly sized ovenproof dish. Pile the mixture into this and press down lightly.

3 Bake in an oven preheated to 180°C/350°F/Gas Mark 4 for 1¹/₄hours. Turn out carefully, as there will be some juice, and serve at once, or allow to cool and serve cold.

CORNED BEEF HASH

Everybody who makes this dish probably includes a slight varia-tion. This recipe is basic and simple, great if you have some left-over cold, cooked potatoes, but certainly worth cooking some for if you do not.

Preparation time: 25 minutes
Cooking time: 25 minutes

You will need:

700g (1¹/₄lb) potatoes

350g (12oz) can corned beef, ideally kept in the fridge for a couple of hours

30ml (2tbspn) vegetable oil

1 large onion, chopped

45ml (3tbspn) Worcestershire sauce

Salt and pepper

1 Peel the potatoes and cut into evenly-sized chunks. Place in a pan, cover with cold water and add 5ml (1tspn) of salt. Place on a hob on a high heat and bring to the boil. Reduce the heat and simmer for about 20 minutes, or until the potatoes are just tender when pierced with a sharp knife. If anything, it is better to slightly undercook them, as they will be easier to dice. Drain and cool slightly.

2 When cool enough to handle, cut the potatoes into cubes about 2cm (³/₄inch) along each side.

3 Meanwhile, carefully take the corned beef out of the tin. Cut it into 1cm (¹/₂ inch) cubes, which the chilling should make easier.

4 Heat the oil in a large pan over a medium to high heat. Add the onion and cook for 5 minutes, stirring, until it just starts to brown.

5 Pile in the potatoes and corned beef and cook for 10–15 minutes, turning over the mixture with a wooden spoon from

time to time. The potatoes should start to brown and the corned beef will begin to break up.

6 Pour in the Worcestershire sauce and mix well. Season to taste and serve at once.

SAVOURY BATTER

A basic batter is the starting point for many dishes – toad-in-the-hole, Yorkshire puddings and pancakes spring immediately to mind – but sweet batters, made like toad-in-the-hole but using fruit instead of meat can also be made (see page 187).

BASIC BATTER
110g (4oz) plain flour
Pinch of salt
1egg
175ml (10 fl oz) milk

1 Sieve the flour and salt into a large bowl and push the mixture up at the sides to make a well in the centre

2 Crack the egg into the well with about one third of the milk and stir them together in the centre of the flour with a wooden spoon.

3 Using a circular motion, stir the mixture, pulling in a little more of the flour each time. As the mixture gets thicker with the addition of the flour, gradually add more milk.

4 When all the flour is mixed in, add the rest of the milk and swap your wooden spoon for a whisk. Beat the mixture well for a few minutes until it is very smooth, with bubbles on top. If your mixture is a bit lumpy, pour it through a sieve into another bowl, pushing through the lumps with a wooden spoon, and then whisk well.

5 Allow the mixture to stand for at least half an hour. This allows the flour to swell and thicken the mixture slightly. You can actually make the batter several hours in advance, just give it a quick stir before you want to use it.

TOAD-IN-THE-HOLE

Preparation time: 10 minutes + standing
Cooking time: 40 minutes

You will need:
1 quantity of basic batter mix (page 145)
8 large sausages

1 Make the batter as directed.

2 Arrange the sausages over the base of an ovenproof dish, large enough to allow them to lie in a single layer. Place the dish in an oven preheated to 220°C/425°F/Gas Mark 7 for about 8–10 minutes, until the sausages are starting to brown and some of their fat has run out.

3 Quickly pour the batter over the sausages. It should sizzle a bit. Return the dish to the oven for 25–30 minutes, until the batter is well risen, crispy and golden brown. Serve at once.

Cook's Tip

Instead of sausages, you could use a combination of lightly cooked vegetables. Courgettes, sweetcorn, onions, mushrooms and leeks all work well. Heat 30ml (2tbspn) of vegetable oil in the dish for 10 minutes, then add the vegetables and batter and proceed as above.

YORKSHIRE PUDDINGS

I like to cook these in bun tins to make individual puddings, but you can cook the mixture in one large dish.

Makes: 12 small or 1 large pudding
Preparation time: 10 minutes + standing
Cooking time: 15–30 minutes, depending on size

You will need:
1 quantity of basic batter mix (page 145)
Vegetable oil

1 Make the batter as directed and transfer to a jug.

2 Put a drop of oil in the bottom of each bun tin, or 30ml (2tbspn) of oil in a large tin, and place in an oven preheated to 220°C/425°F/Gas Mark 7 for 5–7 minutes, until the fat is literally smoking hot. Be very careful as you handle the hot tin and fat. Very quickly pour in the batter and you should see it sizzle and actually start to cook around the edges. Return to the oven and cook for 15–20 minutes for small puddings, or 25–30 minutes for a large one.

3 Serve with roast beef or use mini puds as containers for chilli or curry. Any spare pudding is delicious for dessert with golden syrup or jam drizzled over the top.

PASTA AND SAUCES

There is now a huge variety of pasta available in shops, both fresh and dried and in an amazing choice of shapes and colours. The individual packets will give cooking instructions for the pasta itself. Below are a few ideas for sauces and dressings to serve with it. All the suggestions will be enough to serve 4, for which you will need about 350–450g (12oz–1lb) of pasta, uncooked weight.

GORGONZOLA SAUCE

Preparation time: 5 minutes
Cooking time: 5 minutes

You will need:
225g (8oz) gorgonzola cheese
275ml (10 fl oz) single cream
Salt and pepper

1 Depending on the ripeness of your cheese, either grate, crumble or roughly chop the gorgonzola.

2 Place the cream in a pan over a medium heat and, when hot, add the cheese.

3 Heat gently, stirring, until the cheese has melted, then season to taste. Be cautious with the salt, as gorgonzola can be quite salty, but add plenty of pepper. Pour over freshly cooked and drained pasta.

PESTO AND BLACK PEPPER SAUCE

Simply add 60ml (4tbspn) of pesto and a sprinkling of freshly ground pepper to the drained, cooked pasta and mix thoroughly.

CARBONARA SAUCE

Preparation time: 10 minutes
Cooking time: 10 minutes

You will need:

225g (8oz) good quality ham or bacon
4 eggs
25g (1oz) cheese – grated parmesan is best but cheddar is fine

60ml (4tbspn) single cream
Salt and pepper
50g (2oz) butter

1 Cut the ham or bacon into pieces about 2.5cm (1 inch) square.

2 In a bowl, beat together the eggs, cheese, cream and a good pinch of salt and pepper, until well mixed.

3 Place the butter in a pan over a medium heat. Add the ham or bacon and cook for 4–5 minutes, turning with a wooden spoon, until lightly browned.

4 Add the egg mixture and cook, stirring, until the mixture just begins to thicken, then pour immediately over freshly cooked and drained pasta and stir well. The idea is that the eggs will finish cooking in the heat of the pasta, so it is always better to err on the side of caution when heating the ham and egg mix, or you will have a scrambled-egg sauce.

GARLIC AND OLIVE OIL SAUCE

Pasta sauces do not have to be elaborate. This one could not be simpler and is one of the best. Crush a couple of large cloves of garlic. Heat 75ml (5tbspn) of olive oil in a pan over a medium heat. Add the crushed garlic and cook until it just starts to brown. Add a generous helping of freshly ground black pepper. Pour over freshly cooked and drained pasta, toss together and serve at once.

RISOTTO

A classic risotto uses a special rice that has very fat grains. It is cooked by slowly adding hot stock and allowing it to be absorbed before adding more. The finished dish has an almost creamy consistency and a slight bite to the rice. The following recipe is not a classic but is a quick and easy meal-in-a-pan. It's a delicious, if not authentic, dish that you can vary as you wish.

Preparation time: 10 minutes
Cooking time: 30 minutes

You will need:

90ml (6tbspn) vegetable oil

1 large onion, finely chopped

2 cloves garlic, crushed

110g (4oz) button mushrooms, chopped

350g (12oz) long grain rice

570ml (1pt) boiling water

2 vegetable stock cubes

400g (14oz) can chopped tomatoes in juice

Salt and pepper

110g (4oz) cheddar cheese, grated

1 Heat the oil in a large pan over a medium heat. Add the onion and garlic and cook, stirring, for 5 minutes.

2 Add the mushrooms and cook for a couple more minutes, then add the rice and stir it around in the onion mixture for a few minutes until it is well coated with oil and looks glossy.

3 Now dissolve the stock cubes in the water and add to the pan with the contents of the can of tomatoes. Stir well, reduce the heat to low, and cook gently for about 20 minutes, until the rice is just tender. Stir the mixture occasionally, so it does not stick to the bottom of the pan. When the rice is cooked, most of the liquid should be absorbed. If it looks too wet, turn up the heat for a few minutes to evaporate some of the liquid. On the other hand, if the pan looks rather dry before the rice is cooked, simply pour in a little more boiling water.

4 Remove the pan from the heat, stir in the cheese and season.

VARIATIONS

Try adding one or a combination of several of the following ingredients about 5 minutes before the end of the cooking time.

225g (8oz) cooked, shelled prawns, defrosted and drained if frozen.

225g (8oz) cooked chicken or ham, cut into 1cm ($1/2$ inch) cubes.

225g (8oz) sliced salami or garlic sausage, cut into strips.

A small can of sweetcorn, drained.

A small can of tuna or salmon, drained.

A small red and green pepper, deseeded and roughly chopped.

The recipe uses white rice. For a nuttier flavour, replace this with long grain brown rice. This takes about twice as long to cook, so you probably need to add more water during the cooking time.

LEEK AND BEAN PAN-FRY

This is one of those splendid meals where everything is cooked together in one pan, which saves time, fuel and, most importantly, washing up! Some fresh, crusty bread is a good accompaniment.

Preparation time: 15 minutes
Cooking time: 35 minutes

You will need:

30ml (2tbspn) vegetable oil

2 onions, chopped

2 leeks, cut into 5mm (¹/₄ inch) slices and
   thoroughly washed

350g (12oz) minced beef

420g (15oz) can baked beans

175g (6oz) cheddar cheese, grated

1 tomato, sliced

Salt and pepper

1 Put the oil in a large frying pan over a medium heat. Add the onions, leeks and mince and cook, stirring, for 20 minutes.

2 Add the beans and half the cheese, lower the heat and cook for 3–4 minutes. Meanwhile, preheat the grill to high.

3 Season the mix with salt and pepper to taste.

4 Give the mixture in the pan a final stir, then level it roughly, sprinkle with the remaining cheese, and arrange the tomato slices over the top. Put the pan under the grill, being careful not to heat the handle, and heat until the cheese is bubbling. Serve as soon as possible.

ITALIAN LIVER

Some people will immediately turn over when they see the word liver, but it is a relatively cheap and nutritious meat and this way of presenting it turns it into a delicious treat, served with rice, potatoes or pasta.

Preparation time: 10 minutes + soaking
Cooking time: 40 minutes

You will need:

275g (10oz) liver (lamb or ox)
275ml (10 fl oz) milk
25g (1oz) plain flour
Salt and pepper
45ml (3tbspn) vegetable oil
450g (1lb) onions, peeled, halved and
    thinly sliced

150ml (5 fl oz) water
1 beef or vegetable stock cube
30ml (2tbspn) tomato purée
1 clove garlic, crushed
Pinch of mixed herbs or Italian seasoning

1 Cut the liver into strips about 2.5cm (1 inch) wide. Place in a shallow dish and cover with the milk. Leave to soak for an hour, then lift out the liver and keep the milk.

2 Mix the flour with 5ml (1tspn) of salt and a good pinch of pepper on a piece of kitchen paper (see Cook's tip below). Dip the pieces of liver into the seasoned flour until they are all evenly coated.

3 Heat the oil in a frying pan over a medium to high heat. Fry the liver until browned, then turn over and brown the other side. Remove from the pan and leave on a plate.

4 Add the onions to the pan and fry gently for 10 minutes. Add the water, crumbled stock cube, reserved milk, tomato purée, garlic and herbs. Bring the mixture to the boil, stirring.

5 Return the liver to the pan, reduce the heat and simmer for 15–20 minutes until the liver is just cooked. Do not be tempted to overcook this dish, as the liver will become tough.

6 Add salt and pepper to taste. If you wish, you could sprinkle a little chopped, fresh parsley over the top of the dish before serving, to add a little colour.

Cook's Tip

Mixing salt and pepper into the flour gives "seasoned flour". This is used to coat pieces of meat, usually when they are to be quickly browned before further cooking. The flour has three purposes: it adds flavour; it helps the meat to brown; and it also helps to thicken the gravy.

BEEF AND ONION PATTIES

These are a bit like fishcakes but made with corned beef. This is another recipe that is easily cooked in one pan, and a side-order of baked beans makes the perfect accompaniment.

Preparation time: 15 minutes
Cooking time: 15 minutes

You will need:

60g (2¹/₂oz) packet instant mashed potato
150ml (5 fl oz) milk
150ml (5 fl oz) hot water
Large can corned beef
1 onion, finely chopped
Salt and pepper

110g (4oz) fresh white breadcrumbs (see Cook's tip)
15ml (1tbspn) Worcestershire sauce
2.5ml (¹/₂tspn) mustard powder
3 eggs
Vegetable oil for frying

1 Make up the potato, using the milk and water as suggested on the packet.

2 Place the corned beef in a bowl and mash roughly, using a fork. Mix into the potato with the onion, breadcrumbs, Worcestershire sauce, mustard powder and eggs.

3 Add a little salt and pepper and beat well with a wooden spoon until thoroughly mixed. Don't worry that the mixture looks rather unappetising at this stage.

4 Heat about 30ml (2tbspn) of oil in a frying pan over a medium heat. Drop large spoonfuls of the mixture into the pan and fry for 3–4 minutes. Flip the cakes over using a palette knife or fish slice and cook for a further 3–4 minutes on the other side until firm and golden.

5 Remove the cakes to a plate and keep warm under a low grill while you cook the rest of the mix.

Cook's Tip

Making breadcrumbs is easy if you have a blender or food processor. Simply tear the bread into rough chunks, pop into the machine, put the lid on and blend for a few seconds. If you don't have one of these handy machines, arm yourself with a cheese-grater. Rub the bread (unsliced, slightly stale bread is best for this operation) against the roughest side of the grater, keeping nails and knuckles at a safe distance. You may like to make a large batch of breadcrumbs while you are about it and store them in a bag in the freezer for future use.

FRANKFURTER AND BEAN HOTPOT

I am a great fan of recipes that can be cooked in one pan and this dish falls into that category. It can be served with crusty bread or baked potatoes for a hearty supper dish. Vary the meat as you wish – left-over cooked sausages go well in this dish.

Preparation time: 10 minutes
Cooking time: 30 minutes

25g (1oz) butter
1 large onion, chopped
4 rashers of bacon, any type, roughly chopped
8 frankfurters, tinned or chilled, cut into 1cm (1/2 inch) lengths
110g (4oz) garlic sausage, roughly chopped
2 x 400g (14oz) cans red kidney beans, drained and rinsed
150ml (5 fl oz) water
1 vegetable or chicken stock cube
Salt and pepper
30ml (2tbspn) fresh parsley, chopped

1 Melt the butter in a large saucepan over a medium heat. Add the onion and bacon and fry, stirring, until the onion is softened and the bacon golden brown – about 10 minutes.

2 Add the frankfurters, garlic sausage, beans, water and stock cube. Stir well, lower the heat and cook gently for 20 minutes, stirring every 5 minutes or so to ensure that the mixture does not stick to the base of the pan.

3 Season, stir in the parsley and serve at once.

SAUSAGE SIZZLE

Concentrated soups make a good base for a sauce. Mushroom works particularly well, not just in this recipe but in chicken casserole, over fish or mixed with chopped ham over a jacket potato or pasta.

Preparation time: 10 minutes
Cooking time: 40 minutes

15ml (1tbspn) vegetable oil
2 large onions, chopped
4 rashers bacon, roughly chopped
450g (1lb) pork sausages (should be 8)
Half a 300g (11oz) can condensed
    mushroom soup

215ml (7.5 fl oz) water
Pinch of mixed herbs
Salt and pepper

1 Heat the oil in a large frying pan over a medium heat. Add the onion and cook, stirring occasionally, until beginning to tinge brown – about 10 minutes.

2 Push the onion to one side of the pan, add the bacon and cook, stirring, for 5 minutes.

3 Remove the onion and bacon from the pan and keep on a plate. Add the sausages and fry for about 12–15 minutes, until well browned, turning frequently. Take the sausages out of the pan and cut each one across into 4 pieces.

4 Return the onion, bacon and sausages to the pan. Add the soup, water and herbs and stir to mix well. Bring to the boil, then reduce the heat and simmer for 10 minutes. Season to taste and serve with baked potatoes, rice or pasta, and a green vegetable.

BEEF STEW AND DUMPLINGS

Below is a basic stew recipe. Obviously, you can adjust the vegetables to your taste – you could add turnip or parsnip instead of the swede and perhaps sliced leek instead of the pepper. A small tin of sweetcorn or some frozen peas might also be added, and adding a can of kidney beans would probably stretch the dish to serve 6 people. The dumplings are optional but will greatly enhance your reputation as a cook – everybody secretly loves them.

Preparation time: 30 minutes
Cooking time: 2¹/₂ hours

You will need:

560g (1¹/4lb) stewing beef, cut into
    2cm (³/4 inch) cubes
30ml (2tbspn) plain flour
Salt and pepper
30ml (2tbspn) vegetable oil
3 carrots, peeled and cut into
    5mm (¹/4 inch) slices

1 large onion, chopped
1 small swede, peeled and cut into
    approximately 1cm (¹/2 inch) cubes
1 small red pepper, deseeded and cut into
    strips about 5mm (¹/4 inch) wide
425ml (15 fl oz) water
2 beef stock cubes

DUMPLINGS

110g (4oz) self-raising flour
50g (2oz) suet

Pinch of salt
Cold water to mix

1 Mix the flour with a large pinch of salt and pepper and toss the cubes of beef in this until they are well coated.

2 Heat the oil in a large pan over a medium to high heat, about 10 cubes at a time, turning until lightly browned all over. When one batch is browned, remove it from the pan and keep on a plate while browning the next lot. Two or three minutes for each batch is all that is needed – you are sealing the juices into the meat and adding colour, but not trying to cook it.

3 When you have removed the last batch of meat, add the vegetables to the pan, adding a little more oil if necessary, and quickly stir them around in the pan for 3–4 minutes.

4 Transfer the meat and vegetables to a casserole dish. Add the water, crumble in the stock cubes and stir well. Cover with a well-fitting lid or a double layer of foil and place the casserole in an oven preheated to 180°C/350°F/Gas Mark 4 for about 2–2¹/4 hours, until the meat and vegetables are tender.

5 To make the dumplings, place the flour, suet and salt in a bowl and slowly add the water, mixing with a knife and then your hands until you have a ball of soft but not sticky dough and no loose flour left in the bowl.

6 Divide the mixture into 8 pieces and shape each one into a ball. Place the balls evenly over the top of the stew, re-cover and return to the oven for about 20–25 minutes. If you like crispy-topped dumplings, remove the casserole lid after 10 minutes.

VARIATIONS

Replace half the water and one stock cube with beer. Instead of dumplings, spread 2cm (3/4 inch) thick slices of French stick with mustard, place on top of the casserole, slightly overlapping them, and cook for 15 minutes, without a lid.

Instead of beef, use diced chicken – boneless thigh works well – and chicken stock cubes rather than beef. Cook for 1 1/2 hours.

SAVOURY MINCE

This recipe provides a basis for many meals, some of which are mentioned as alternatives below. You can use any type of mince, as discussed on page 43, but beef mince (with 10–15% fat) will give good results.

Preparation time: 5 minutes
Cooking time: 25 minutes

You will need:

450 g (1 lb) mince	1 beef stock cube
1 large onion, finely chopped	5 ml (1 tspn) salt
15 ml (1 tbspn) vegetable oil	Good pinch of pepper
150 ml (5 fl oz) water	10ml (2tspn) cornflour

1 Place the onions and mince with the oil in a large pan over a medium heat. Prod well with a wooden spoon to mix the meat and onions and to break up the mince as it starts to cook.

2 When the meat begins to cook – about 5 minutes – add the water and stir well until the liquid starts to bubble (simmer).

3 Sprinkle in the stock cube and stir until dissolved. Now lower the heat and let the mixture bubble gently for 15–20 minutes.

4 Add the salt and pepper and stir well.

5 Mix the cornflour with 30ml (2tbspn) of cold water and, stirring the meat mixture all the time, pour in the cornflour paste. You will find that the mixture thickens and looks clearer.

This basic recipe can be adapted in many ways. Reduce or increase the quantities depending upon how many people you have to feed and remember, if you have a freezer, it's economical to make a large batch and freeze part of it. Try adding a crushed clove of garlic or roughly chopped mushrooms at stage 1.

BOLOGNESE SAUCE

You will need:
Savoury mince recipe (page 161)
400g (14oz) can chopped tomatoes in juice
2.5ml (¹/₂tspn) Italian seasoning
15ml (1tbspn) tomato purée

Use the tomatoes and juice instead of water and add the seasoning and tomato purée with the stock cube. Continue with the basic recipe.

SHEPHERD'S PIE

You will need:
Savoury mince recipe (page 161)   Butter
450g (1lb) potatoes, peeled   Salt and pepper
Milk

1 Make the basic recipe, though you might like to add a little more cornflour paste to make the gravy slightly thicker. Turn into an ovenproof dish.

2 Meanwhile, boil and mash about 450 g (1 lb) of potatoes (see page 121), being sure to add seasoning and plenty of milk and butter to make them creamy.

3 Carefully spread the mashed potato over the top of the mince, spreading it out to totally cover the meat. A nice touch is to ridge the potato, all over, with a fork, to give a pattern on top.

4 Place the dish in an oven preheated to 220°C/425°F/Gas Mark 7 for 20–25 minutes, until the top is golden and crisp.

CHILLI CON CARNE

You will need:
Savoury mince recipe (page 161)
Clove of garlic, crushed
400g (14oz) can chopped tomatoes in juice
5ml (1tspn) chilli powder
400g (14oz) can red kidney beans, drained
15ml (1tbspn) tomato purée

Make the basic recipe, adding the garlic with the onion. Instead of water, use the tomatoes in juice. Add the chilli powder with the stock cube – you can alter the quantity if you like, depending on how hot you like your chilli and how strong your chilli powder is, but if you're unsure, err on the side of caution. Also add the red kidney beans and tomato purée at this stage. Continue with the basic recipe and simmer for 30 minutes. This mixture should not need thickening with cornflour.

VEGETABLE COBBLER

Do not wait until you are entertaining a vegetarian to try this hearty dish. It is literally a meal in a pot – only the biggest appetites would also require a baked potato. You should find that nearly all cheddar cheese nowadays is suitable for vegetarians, but do check just in case.

Preparation time: 45 minutes
Cooking time: 25 minutes

You will need:

1 large onion	15ml (1tbspn) vegetable oil
225g (8oz) leeks	25g (1oz) plain flour
450g (1lb) carrots	10ml (2tspn) made mustard
1 green pepper	150ml (5 fl oz) orange juice
1 red pepper	275ml (10 fl oz) milk
225g (8oz) courgettes	150ml (5 fl oz) natural yoghurt
25g (1oz) butter	Pinch of salt and pepper

SCONE TOPPING

225g (8oz) self-raising flour	75g (3oz) cheddar cheese, grated
5ml (1tspn) mustard powder	About 150ml (5 fl oz) milk
50g (2oz) margarine	

1 First prepare the vegetables. Peel and thinly slice the onion. Trim the leeks, cut into 2cm ($^3/_4$ inch) chunks and wash and drain thoroughly. Peel the carrots and cut into 5mm ($^1/_4$ inch) slices. Cut the peppers in half, remove the seeds and slice. Trim the ends off the courgettes and cut into 1cm ($^1/_2$ inch) slices.

2 Heat the butter and oil in a large pan over a medium heat. Add the vegetables and fry gently, stirring occasionally, for about 10 minutes, until they are beginning to soften. Then

sprinkle the flour over and cook for a further minute, stirring all the time.

3   Add the mustard, orange juice and milk, increase the heat and stir continuously until the mixture thickens. Now reduce the heat, cover the pan and simmer for about 10 minutes or until the vegetables are tender. Test the carrots, as these generally take the longest to cook.

4   Meanwhile, make the topping. Sieve the flour and mustard powder into a large bowl. Add the margarine, cut into small pieces and rub the fat and flour between your fingers until no large lumps remain. Stir in the cheese. Start adding the milk, stirring with a knife as you do so, to form a dough. It should be soft but not sticky. Knead gently so it looks smooth.

5   Once the vegetables are tender, stir in the yoghurt and transfer the mixture to a large ovenproof dish.

6   Roll out the topping on a floured work-surface to about 1cm ($^1/_2$ inch) thick. Cut into rounds about 5cm (2 inches) across, using a cutter, glass or mug. Knead together the trimmings and re-roll and shape. Arrange the scones, slightly overlapping, in a ring around the top of the vegetables. Brush the top of the scones with milk.

7   Bake in an oven preheated to 220°C/425°F/Gas Mark 7 for 25 minutes, until the scones are puffed up and golden brown.

CHEESE PUDDING

This is a splendid recipe, quick and simple to make, and yet it behaves just like a cheese soufflé and looks most impressive when it comes out of the oven. Like a soufflé, it needs to be eaten at once, perhaps with a green salad, so assemble your "eaters" about 5 minutes before the end of cooking time.

Preparation time: 15 minutes
Cooking time: 35–40 minutes

You will need:

570ml (1pt) milk	4 eggs
50g (2oz) fresh breadcrumbs (see page 156)	Pinch of mustard powder
225g (8oz) cheddar cheese, grated	Pinch of salt and pepper

1 Place the milk in a saucepan over a high heat until just about boiling.

2 Place the breadcrumbs in a bowl and pour over the milk. Mix in the cheese.

3 Beat the eggs in a small bowl with the mustard powder, salt and pepper, and mix into the breadcrumbs.

4 Pour the mixture into a greased casserole dish, about 1.5 litre (2¹/₂pt) capacity and bake in an oven preheated to 180°C/350°F/Gas Mark 4 for about 35–40 minutes until well risen, lightly set and golden brown. It should still have a bit of a wobble, which results in a creamy centre to the dish. Serve at once.

VEGETABLE CURRY

The experienced and enthusiastic curry-maker will have a cupboard full of various seeds and ground spices, all considered essential to a good curry, and doubtless they will produce a great dish ... but so does a jar of good curry paste, and it takes up a lot less space. There are several brands and strengths available and everybody will have their favourite – just experiment a little until you find yours.

Preparation time: 30 minutes
Cooking time: 25–30 minutes

You will need:

1 small cauliflower	1 large onion, peeled and roughly chopped
2 carrots	2 cloves garlic, crushed
4 courgettes	30ml (2tbspn) medium curry paste
1 small green pepper	15ml (1tbspn) tomato purée
110g (4oz) button mushrooms	Boiling water
110g (4oz) french beans	400g (14oz) can chickpeas, drained
4 tomatoes	125g (4¹/₂oz) canned sweetcorn, drained
30ml (2tbspn) vegetable oil	60ml (4tbspn) natural yoghurt

1 Begin by preparing the vegetables. Cut the cauliflower in half, cut out the stalk and cut into florets, then trim these into smaller florets about 1cm (¹/₂ inch) across. Peel the carrots and cut into 5mm (¹/₄ inch) slices. Trim the ends off the courgettes and cut into 5mm (¹/₄ inch) slices. Deseed the green pepper and cut into 1cm (¹/₂ inch) squares. Cut the mushrooms into slices about 5mm (¹/₂ inch) wide. Top and tail the beans and cut into 2cm (³/₄ inch) lengths. Peel the tomatoes (see page 125) and chop roughly.

2 Now heat the oil in a large pan (a frying pan with a lid works well but is not essential) over a medium heat. Add the onion and garlic and cook for 5 minutes, stirring.

3 Add the cauliflower, carrots, courgettes, pepper, mushrooms, beans and tomatoes. Stir into the onions until well mixed.

4 Spoon the curry paste into the pan and roughly mix into the vegetables to disperse it. Add about 150ml (5 fl oz) of boiling water to the pan with the tomato purée, stir well and simmer for about 15 minutes. The water will start to boil away, so keep topping it up but don't be tempted to put more in to start with, as you might make the sauce too runny.

5 The vegetables should be just about tender. If they are not, add a little more water, cover the pan and cook a little longer.

6 Add the chickpeas and sweetcorn, mix well and heat for a further 2–3 minutes. The sauce should be quite thick, so if it isn't, turn up the heat and bubble off some of the liquid. Stir in the yoghurt and heat through gently.

7 When hot, serve with rice or naan bread.

Cook's Tip

Of course, you can adjust the curry paste to your own taste and change the vegetables as well. You could add diced aubergine, frozen peas, spinach, diced potatoes and even diced apples and a handful of sultanas. A sprinkling of flaked almonds and chopped fresh coriander makes an elegant and tasty garnish to this dish.

HADDOCK IN CIDER

Remember, you can buy small bottles or cans of cider so you do not have to waste any! Haddock fillets work well for this recipe, having a good flavour and a reasonably firm flesh, but do not use the smoked variety. Your fishmonger will skin the fish for you if you ask.

Preparation time: 15 minutes
Cooking time: 40 minutes

You will need:

700g (1¹/₂lb) haddock fillets, skinned	Pinch salt and pepper
2 eating apples	275ml (10 fl oz) dry cider
2 stalks celery	10ml (2tspn) cornflour
Vegetable oil	15ml (1tbspn) cold water
5ml (1tspn) chopped fresh sage or parsley	

1 Cut the fish into chunks about 2.5cm (1 inch) square. Leave the skin on the apples, cut into quarters and carefully cut out the core. Cut each wedge into slices about 5mm (¹/₂ inch) thick. Cut the celery into slices about 5mm (¹/₂ inch) thick.

2 Brush a casserole dish with oil and lay in the fish. Cover with the apples and celery, then sprinkle with the sage or parsley and salt and pepper. Pour over the cider and cover the dish with a lid or a double layer of foil crimped around the edges of the dish to make a good seal.

3 Place the dish in an oven preheated to 180°C/350°F/Gas Mark 4 for 30–35 minutes.

4 Meanwhile, mix the cornflour and water together in a small saucepan. When the fish is cooked, use a slotted spoon to transfer it to a serving dish with the apple and celery pieces to keep warm.

5 Slowly add the cooking liquid to the pan with the cornflour mixture, stirring all the time. Place the pan on a high heat and bring to the boil, still stirring continuously, until the sauce has thickened. Pour over the fish and serve at once. Rice or mashed potatoes and broccoli make good accompaniments.

TUNA OR SALMON FISHCAKES

I think that for fishcakes it is worth going to the effort of mashing your own potatoes, as they give a better flavour and texture than instant mash, though if time is pressing, this makes a perfectly acceptable substitute.

Makes: 6 fishcakes
Preparation time: 30 minutes + cooling
Cooking time: 10 minutes

You will need:

450g (1lb) old potatoes, peeled and cut into even-sized chunks
Salt
45ml (3tbspn) milk
25g (1oz) butter

Pepper
185g (6¹/₂oz) can tuna or salmon, drained
Plain flour
Vegetable oil for frying

1 Place the potatoes in a pan, cover with cold water and add 5ml (1tspn) salt. Bring to the boil over a high heat, then reduce the heat and simmer for 20–25 minutes, until the potato pieces feel tender when pierced with a sharp knife. Drain and mash the potatoes with a masher or fork and mix in the milk, butter and a good pinch of pepper. Allow to cool slightly.

2 Empty the fish into a bowl, removing skin and bones, and break up with a fork. Add the potatoes and mix together well.

3 Scoop the mixture out on to a work-surface and divide into 6 fairly evenly-sized pieces. Shape into rounds about 2cm (3/4 inch) thick, using a little flour to prevent sticking. Ensure each cake is floured top and bottom, as this will also help to give a crispy shell when they are fried.

5 Heat about 30ml (2tbspn) oil in a frying pan over a medium to high heat. Add the fishcakes and cook for about 5 minutes, until the base is crisp and golden. Flip the cakes over with a palette knife or fish slice and cook the other side for a further 5 minutes.

6 Serve at once with peas or another vegetable of your choice.

PRAWN AND RICE SALAD

The word salad is deceptive here, as this recipe makes a hearty meal. Obviously you can be flexible with the ingredients, and a few cooked peas, a drained small can of sweetcorn, or some cubed cheddar cheese could be substituted as you wish.

Preparation time: 25 minutes + cooling

You will need:

175g (6oz) long grain white rice
425ml (15 fl oz) water
Pinch of salt
60ml (4tbspn) olive oil
15ml (1tbspn) vinegar
2.5ml (1/2tspn) mustard powder
2.5ml (1/2tspn) caster sugar
Salt and pepper

225g (8oz) shelled, cooked prawns, defrosted and drained if frozen
225g (8oz) cooked chicken, cut into 2cm (3/4 inch) cubes
110g (4oz) button mushrooms
2 dessert apples
About half a small lettuce, shredded, or a bag of prepared lettuce

1 Place the rice, water and pinch of salt in a large saucepan over a high heat. Cover, bring to the boil, then reduce the heat and simmer for 15 minutes, or until the rice is tender. Drain if all the water has not been absorbed by the time the rice is cooked.

2 Put the oil, vinegar, mustard powder, sugar and a pinch of salt and pepper in a small jam jar, screw on the lid and shake to combine all the ingredients. Alternatively, place everything in a small bowl and whisk with a fork. Pour the dressing over the warm rice and mix well. Leave to cool.

3 Meanwhile, slice the mushrooms and cut the skin-on apples into quarters. Cut away the cores and slice the quarters into about 4 pieces.

4 When the rice is cooked, fluff it up with a fork to separate the grains and mix in the prawns, chicken, mushrooms and apples.

5 Place the lettuce in the bottom of a serving dish and top with the rice mixture. Serve as soon as possible.

FISH PIE

This is a bit of a cheat's recipe, but convenience foods should live up to their name. There is quite a range of cod-in-sauce products available in supermarket freezer cabinets – cheese, butter, parsley and mushroom sauces are just some of the flavours – and these would all work well in this dish.

Preparation time: 30 minutes
Cooking time: 20 minutes

You will need:

4 individual packets of cod-in-sauce
700g (1¹/₂lb) potatoes, peeled and cut
   into even-sized chunks

75ml (5tbspn) milk
50g (2oz) butter
Salt and pepper

1 Cook the cod according to the directions on the packet – usually this is a boil-in-the-bag technique.

2 Meanwhile, boil the potatoes. Place them in a large pan, cover with water and add 5ml (1tspn) salt. Place on a high heat, bring to the boil, and then reduce the heat and simmer for about 20 minutes, or until the potatoes feel soft when pierced with a sharp knife. If you are feeling frugal and have a large enough pan, you could cook the potatoes in the bottom of the saucepan in which you are cooking the bags of cod.

3 When the potatoes are tender, drain and mash them with the milk and butter to give a smooth and creamy consistency, adding more milk if necessary to achieve this. Add salt and pepper to taste.

4 When the cod is cooked, carefully empty the sachets into a bowl, when you will discover that the least convenient thing about them is actually getting them out of their bags! With a fork, break up the pieces of fish and blend them with the sauce.

5 Tip the fish into an ovenproof dish, then carefully spoon the potato over the fish and spread it out evenly. If you are too heavy-handed, the potatoes will become submerged under the sauce, which would be interesting, but not quite what you are trying to achieve.

6 Place in an oven preheated to 200°C/400°F/Gas Mark 6 for about 20 minutes, until the top is golden brown and crispy.

TUNA FISH PIE

A friend introduced me to this dish when we shared digs at college. The ingredients sound rather a strange combination, but the resulting dish is quite delicious and another of those wonderful meals cooked in a single pot.

Preparation time: 15 minutes
Cooking time: 25–30 minutes

You will need:

185g (6¹/2oz) can tuna chunks in oil or brine, drained

420g (15oz) can baked beans

Medium-sized packet instant mashed potato

25g (1oz) butter

50g (2oz) cheddar cheese, grated

1 Make up the instant mashed potato as directed on the packet and mix in the butter.

2 Spread the tuna over the base of an ovenproof dish, breaking up any large chunks with a fork. Cover evenly with the baked beans. Pile the mashed potato on top of the beans, ensuring that they are totally covered. Sprinkle the cheese over the top.

3 Place in an oven preheated to 200°C/400°F/Gas Mark 6 for 25–30 minutes, until piping hot and golden brown on top. Serve at once.

DESSERTS

RECIPES

GINGER PUDDING

This has all the warmth and comfort of an old-fashioned pudding but none of the tedious steaming.

BAKED BANANAS

One of those puddings that appears elegant and complex but is actually simple to make.

JILL'S CHOCOLATE PUDDING

A wonderful recipe that separates during cooking to give a fudgy chocolate sauce topped with a light chocolate sponge.

BREAD AND BUTTER PUDDING

An old-fashioned dessert that is currently enjoying a revival of popularity.

BAKED APPLES

Another old favourite that has stood the test of time, made extra tasty with a fruit and nut filling.

BAKED JAM ROLYPOLY

Talking of old favourites, what could be nicer on a cold winter's day than light suet pastry, oozing with jam and crisp and golden on the outside?

GERMAN APPLE CAKE

A versatile recipe that can be eaten hot with cream or custard as a dessert, or cold for afternoon tea.

UNUSUAL FRUIT CRUMBLE

Oats, butter and sugar combine to make a flapjack-style topping for fruit.

FRUIT BATTER PUDDING

Imagine a sweet toad-in-the-hole, bursting with fruit, and you have this delicious dessert.

SCOTCH PANCAKES

Beautifully fluffy little pancakes just asking to be drizzled with golden syrup or jam.

CARAMEL-TOPPED PEACHES

Juicy peaches, cool under a blanket of cream, have a hot topping of caramelised sugar.

POACHED PEARS

Quartered pears, poached in a wine-based syrup, to serve hot, warm or cold.

BANOFFEE PIE

Bananas, caramel sauce and cream, all contained in a crisp pastry shell – bliss!

FRUITY LAYERS

Layers of fruit and cream, sandwiched between crunchy ginger biscuit crumbs.

CHOCOLATE BANANA CREAMS

The name says it all – chocolate, bananas and cream all combine in this rich dessert.

FRUIT FOOLS

One of the simplest cold puddings, fruit purée is combined with cream or custard.

CHOCOLATE MOUSSE

The classic French dessert, simply made with chocolate and eggs.

FRUIT SALAD

The recipe uses fruit of your choice, mixed with a can of pineapple in natural juice, which does away with the need for making a syrup.

HONEYCOMB MOUSSE

Nobody would guess that the secret ingredient in this delicious dessert is chocolate-covered honeycomb bars.

SYLLABUB

A classic dinner-party pudding, very boozy and delicious, served with crisp biscuits.

CHOCOLATE AND CHESTNUT LOAF

A rich concoction of chocolate, chestnut purée, butter and eggs that combine to make a truly elegant dessert.

GINGER PUDDING

This is a warming and sustaining pudding for a cold winter's day and definitely a candidate for a jug of custard.

Preparation time: 20 minutes
Cooking time: 20 minutes

You will need:

1 large cooking apple
30ml (2tbspn) orange marmalade
50g (2oz) margarine
50g (2oz) caster sugar

1 egg
75g (3oz) self-raising flour
2.5ml (1/2tspn) ground ginger

1 Peel the apple and cut into quarters. Remove the core and cut each piece into thin slices. Place the slices in the base of a shallow ovenproof dish about 20cm (8 inches) in diameter and smear the marmalade over the top as evenly as possible.

2 Place the margarine and sugar together in a bowl and work together with a wooden spoon. When they are combined, beat together until the mixture looks paler and fluffy. Beat in the egg until it has combined with the margarine and sugar. Sift in the flour and ginger and stir into the egg mixture as gently as possible, but ensuring that everything is well blended.

3 Spread this cake mixture carefully over the apples right to the edges of the dish, so that the apple is completely covered.

4 Bake in an oven preheated to 200°C/400°F/Gas Mark 6 for 20 minutes, until the pudding is golden and well risen and feels springy when lightly pressed in the middle.

5 Run a knife around the edge of the dish to loosen the cake, then place a plate over the top of the dish and turn upside down. At this point, the pudding should be sitting, apple side up, on the plate. Serve hot with cream, ice-cream or custard.

BAKED BANANAS

For a simple yet sophisticated dessert, popular with children and adults alike, this cannot be beaten. Make it even more of a favourite with your adult guests by adding a dash of brandy or rum with the orange juice. If such a thing is possible, vanilla ice-cream makes this pudding even tastier.

Preparation time: 15 minutes
Cooking time: 20 minutes

You will need:

25g (1oz) cornflour
90ml (6tbspn) water
90ml (6tbspn) orange juice

110g (4oz) golden syrup
6 bananas
50g (2oz) butter

1 Place the cornflour in a small saucepan, add about half the water and mix to a paste, ensuring that the cornflour is well blended with no lumps. Then mix in the rest of the water, the orange juice and the golden syrup. Place on a medium heat and cook, stirring all the time, until the mixture has thickened. Take off the heat.

2 Peel the bananas and cut in half. Then cut each piece in half lengthways.

3 Smear a little of the butter around the sides and base of an ovenproof dish. Place the banana pieces in the dish and pour the sauce over. Dot with small pieces of the remaining butter.

4 Place in an oven preheated to 180°C/350°F/Gas Mark 4 for 20 minutes. Serve hot.

JILL'S CHOCOLATE PUDDING

This is a splendid dish because, at the end of it, you have a pudding and sauce both cooked in the same dish, with no messy saucepans to wash up. The method sounds a bit odd and you could be forgiven for being doubtful that it will work, but rest assured, it does.

Preparation time: 20 minutes
Cooking time: 40 minutes

You will need:

50g (2oz) butter
75g (3oz) light soft brown sugar
25g (1oz) cocoa powder
75g (3oz) self-raising flour
3 eggs, beaten together in a small bowl
5ml (1tspn) vanilla essence

SAUCE
25g (1oz) cocoa powder
110g (4oz) light soft brown sugar

1 Place the butter in a small saucepan over a very low heat until it just melts. Remove from the heat.

2 Sift the flour and cocoa powder into a bowl and mix in the sugar. Stir in the melted butter, eggs and vanilla essence and mix it all together well with a wooden spoon. Pour the mixture into an ovenproof dish of at least 1.1 litres (2pt) capacity.

3 Now mix the remaining cocoa powder and sugar with 425ml (15 fl oz) of very hot water. Take your nerve in both hands and pour this over the pudding mixture in the dish.

4 Place in an oven preheated to 180°C/350°F/Gas Mark 4 for 35–40 minutes, during which time the pudding will magically separate into a light chocolate sponge with a rich chocolate sauce underneath ... honestly!

BREAD AND BUTTER PUDDING

This dessert used to have a terribly old fashioned, school-dinner feel to it, but recently it has become quite trendy, seen on the menus of several top restaurants.

Preparation time: 15 minutes + standing
Cooking time: 45 minutes

You will need:

6 slices of bread – white is fine
50g (2oz) butter
50g (2oz) currants or sultanas
2 eggs

50g (2oz) caster sugar
570ml (1pt) full-cream milk, or half milk
   and half double cream

1 Lightly grease an ovenproof dish that holds at least 1.1 litres (2pt) and is about 5cm (2 inches) deep.

2 Cut the crusts off the bread and butter each slice quite thickly. Cut each slice either into 4 fingers or 4 smaller squares.

3 Arrange half the bread to cover the base of the dish, butter side up. Sprinkle with the dried fruit and half of the sugar. Cover with the remaining bread, butter side up.

4 Beat the eggs and milk, or milk and cream, together in a bowl or jug until well blended. Then pour evenly over the pudding. Leave to stand for about half an hour, during which time the bread will start to absorb some of the liquid. Now sprinkle with the remaining sugar.

5 Bake in an oven preheated to 180°C/350°F/Gas Mark 4 for about 40–45 minutes until crisp and golden on top and just set. No milk mixture should ooze out if you press the top gently. Serve at once.

BAKED APPLES

Sometimes it is good to revisit old favourites. There is nothing more comforting than a baked apple, particularly one with a gooey filling. Serve this dish warm with cream or ice-cream.

Preparation time: 15 minutes
Cooking time: 45 minutes

You will need:

4 large evenly-sized cooking apples – Bramleys work well
50g (2oz) raisins, glacé cherries, dried apricots, dates, or a mixture
25g (1oz) chopped nuts
2.5ml (1/2tspn) ground cinnamon
50g (2oz) soft brown sugar
25g (1oz) butter

1 Core the apples. This can be done quickly with an apple corer or with a thin bladed knife (watch your fingers). Then run the knife around the centre of each apple, making a slit that just pierces the skin. This stops the apples from bursting as they cook.

2 Chop the dried fruit of your choice into small pieces and combine with the nuts, cinnamon and all but 10ml (2tspn) of the brown sugar.

3 Sit the apples in a well-greased ovenproof dish and divide the stuffing between the middles, pushing it down well. Top each apple with a little butter and a sprinkling of the remaining sugar.

4 Pour a little water into the dish so that it just covers the bottom but does not cover the apples.

5 Place in an oven preheated to 180°C/350°F/Gas Mark 4 for about 40–45 minutes, until the apple is soft if you prod through the slit with a sharp knife. Serve as soon as possible, as the apples will collapse and look less attractive if kept waiting.

BAKED JAM ROLYPOLY

This is an absolutely essential recipe to have in your repertoire because there are certain days in the middle of winter when only a jam rolypoly will do. I would recommend using the stronger flavoured jams, such as blackcurrant or damson, for this dish. Remember, if you are cooking for a vegetarian, non-animal-based suet is readily available in shops.

Preparation time: 20 minutes
Cooking time: 40 minutes

You will need:

225g (8oz) self-raising flour
110g (4oz) suet

Cold water to bind
About 350g (12oz) jam

1 Place the flour and suet in a bowl and mix together. Gradually start adding cold water, stirring the mixture with a knife, until it begins to form a dough. It is easiest then to use your hands and start pulling the dough together, adding a little more water to bind up the loose bits.

2 Turn the mixture on to a floured worktop and knead lightly to form a smooth dough. Roll out into an oblong about 30 x 23cm (12 x 9 inches), keeping the edges as straight as possible. If they become a little ragged, fold them in towards the middle and re-roll. You can also push the edges of the dough with the sides of your hands to keep it in check.

3 When you have the right shape, spread evenly with the jam, covering all the pastry except for a 2cm (3/4 inch) strip along one of the 23cm (9 inch) edges. Fold over the long edges about 2cm (3/4 inch) and brush these edges and the strip not covered with jam with cold water. This will help the pastry to seal.

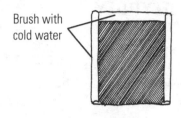
Brush with
cold water

4 Start rolling up from the 23cm (9 inch) jammed end, like a swiss roll. When you are within 10cm (4 inches) of the other end, stop and flip this end over, which will stop the jam being pushed along and forced out at the end. Squeeze together the ends, to seal the jam in, and carefully transfer the rolypoly to a baking tray with the "seam" down.

5 Place in an oven preheated to 200°C/400°F/Gas Mark 6 for about 35–40 minutes, until crisp and golden brown. Serve hot (and remember the jam will be very hot) with custard.

Cook's Tip

Even the greatest cooks will sometimes find that jam boils out when the rolypoly is cooking. Although it will sometimes seem like a flood, don't worry, there will still be plenty of jam left inside. However, it will save a lot of time prising off caramelised jam, if you line your baking tray with greaseproof paper.

GERMAN APPLE CAKE

This is a great recipe that can be eaten hot as a dessert or cold at teatime. You could omit the sultanas or the nuts, but not both.

Preparation time: 20 minutes
Cooking time: 55 minutes

You will need:

450g (1lb) cooking apples, peeled, cored and cut into 1cm (1/2 inch) cubes	2.5ml (3/4tspn) cinnamon
59g (2oz) sultanas	110g (4oz) butter
50g (2oz) demerara sugar	150g (5oz) self-raising flour
50g (2oz) chopped walnuts or flaked almonds	110g (4oz) caster sugar
	1 large egg

1 In a bowl, mix the apples, sultanas, demerara sugar, nuts and cinnamon.

2 In a large pan, melt the butter over a low heat until it is just liquid. Remove from the heat. Using a wooden spoon, stir in the flour, sugar and egg to give a smooth paste.

3 Grease the base of a round ovenproof dish, about 20cm (8 inches) across and then cover the base with a piece of grease-proof paper. A flan dish or shallow cake tin is best for this job, but you can use a casserole dish if necessary.

4 Spread about 2/3 of the cake mixture over the base of the dish as evenly as possible. Then pile the apple mixture over the top, spreading it out evenly to give the same thickness all over.

5 Spoon the remaining cake mixture over the top of the apple in small spoonfuls and spread these out a bit to cover as much of the apple mixture as possible. Don't worry, it is almost impossible to get this very even, but the mixture will spread out as it cooks.

6 Bake in an oven preheated to 180°C/350°F/Gas Mark 4 for 50–55 minutes, until golden brown and firm to the touch. Allow to cool slightly before serving.

UNUSUAL FRUIT CRUMBLE

This is a crumble with a difference, more like a flapjack on fruit. A few chopped nuts stirred into the crumble make an interesting variation. Use any fruit you like, but this is particularly good with sharp fruit like gooseberries and rhubarb.

Preparation time: 15 minutes
Cooking time: 50 minutes

You will need:

700g (1¹/₂lb) fruit of your choice
Sugar to taste
175g (6oz) rolled oats

75g (3oz) butter
75g (3oz) soft brown sugar

1 Prepare the fruit as necessary and cut larger pieces into bite-sized chunks. Place in an ovenproof dish – the fruit should come about halfway up the sides. Sprinkle with sugar. The amount will depend on the fruit you are using, ranging from not much for raspberries to quite a lot for rhubarb.

2 Place the oats, butter and sugar in a bowl and rub together through your fingers to make a crumbly mixture with no big pieces of butter visible. Sprinkle this over the fruit.

3 Place in an oven preheated to 180°C/350°F/Gas Mark 4 for 40–50 minutes, until the fruit is tender and the crumble is golden. Test by piercing through the centre of the crumble with a sharp knife. If the fruit is cooked, you should meet with no resistance.

4 Serve hot with cream or custard.

FRUIT BATTER PUDDING

This is like a sweet version of toad-in-the-hole and an Anglicised version of the classic French dish clafoutis.

Preparation time: 20 minutes + standing
Cooking time: 40 minutes

You will need:

1 quantity basic batter mixture (page 145)	50g (2oz) soft brown sugar
450g (1lb) cooking apples	Caster sugar
25g (1oz) butter	

1 Make the batter as directed and allow to stand.

2 Meanwhile, peel the apples, cut into quarters and cut out the cores. Cut into slices – about three slices from each quarter.

3 Use the butter to grease a shallow ovenproof dish that will hold about 1¹/₂ litres (2¹/₂pt). Place in the apple slices and sprinkle with the brown sugar.

4 Place the dish in an oven preheated to 220°C/425°F/Gas Mark 7 for 10 minutes, then take out, quickly pour over the batter and quickly put back into the oven. Bake for 30 minutes, until well risen, crispy and golden brown.

5 Sprinkle with the caster sugar and serve at once with custard or ice-cream or a drizzling of golden syrup.

VARIATIONS

Try using halved and stoned plums or apricots, raspberries, black-berries or cherries instead of the apples.

SCOTCH PANCAKES

Also known as drop scones, these puffy little pancakes make a delicious pudding, especially if served with golden syrup or jam.

Preparation time: 15 minutes
Cooking time: 10 minutes

You will need:

225g (8oz) plain flour

10ml (2tspn) caster sugar

5ml (1tspn) cream of tartar

2.5ml (1/2tspn) bicarbonate of soda

1 egg

275ml (10 fl oz) milk

Oil for frying

1 Sift the flour, sugar, cream of tartar and bicarbonate of soda into a bowl.

2 Break in the egg and gradually beat in the milk with a wooden spoon to make a thick batter.

3 Heat a little oil – about 15ml (1tbspn) – in a frying pan over a medium to high heat. Drop in 15ml (1tbspn) of the batter in 4 lots. Cook until bubbles start to rise and break on the surface – about 2–3 minutes – then flip the pancakes over with a palette knife. Try to turn them over in the same order as you dropped them into the pan, so that they all cook for the same length of time. Cook until the bases are golden brown.

4 Take the pancakes out of the pan and keep them warm, while you repeat the process and cook the rest of the mixture.

5 Serve hot, with butter, honey, jam or golden syrup.

CARAMEL-TOPPED PEACHES

The secret with this dish is to chill the cream well and then never to take your eyes off the grill when melting the sugar.

Preparation time: 10 minutes + chilling
Cooking time: 5 minutes

You will need:
450g (1lb) can peach halves or slices in natural juice
275ml (10 fl oz) double cream
175g (6oz) demerara sugar

1 Drain the peaches and arrange the fruit over the base of a fairly shallow ovenproof dish.

2 Pour the cream into a bowl and beat with a whisk until it just begins to thicken. Spread it over the peaches, ensuring that all the fruit is covered, and smooth the top as evenly as possible.

3 Chill for at least three hours or overnight if wished.

4 Just before serving, turn the grill to high. Sprinkle the sugar evenly over the cream and slide the dish under the grill, watching it like a hawk until the sugar melts. Serve at once.

VARIATIONS

Try mixing half cream and half Greek yoghurt or crème fraîche. Fresh raspberries or canned apricots also work well in this dish.

POACHED PEARS

This is a great dish to make if you have some fairly average wine, red, white or rosé, left over. Served with whipped cream, it makes an elegant dessert for a dinner party.

Preparation time: 15 minutes
Cooking time: 30–50 minutes

You will need:

8 firm dessert pears
110g (4oz) caster sugar

150ml (5 fl oz) water
275ml (10 fl oz) wine

1 Peel the pears and cut into quarters. Cut out the cores, losing as little of the pears as possible.

2 In a large pan, place the wine, water and sugar and stir over a low heat until the sugar has dissolved.

3 Add the pears. They should be covered by the syrup, so if they are not, add a little more wine or water. Raise the heat and bring the syrup to the boil.

4 Now either reduce the heat and simmer gently for 25 minutes, or you can put the pears in an ovenproof dish and bake in an oven preheated to 190°C/375°F/Gas Mark 5 for about 45 minutes. When cooked, pears can easily be pierced with a sharp knife.

5 Serve hot, warm or cold with cream, custard or ice-cream.

Cook's Tip

The addition of a few cloves, removed before serving, adds an interesting flavour, as does a pinch of ground cinnamon.

BANOFFEE PIE

This is a seriously wicked and terribly trendy dessert. It is also incredibly rich. It is now easy to find pre-baked flan cases in the packaged cake section of supermarkets. Of course, you can make your own, but why make life more difficult? The cooking time seems long, but as you will see from the recipe, it is very easy.

Preparation time: 15 minutes
Cooking time: 3 hours

You will need:

20cm (8 inches) pre-baked pastry flan case

400g (14oz) can condensed milk

2 large bananas

275ml (10 fl oz) double cream

1 First deal with the condensed milk. Peel off the paper label, then place the can, unopened, in a large saucepan and cover well with cold water. Do not put a lid on the pan. Place the pan on a hob heated to its highest setting and bring to the boil. Reduce the heat slightly and simmer for three hours. Because the pan is not covered, you will need to keep topping up the water as it boils away, and it does this surprisingly quickly. The can must always be covered with water. It is a good idea to keep a kettle boiled for this purpose. If you have a large enough saucepan, you can cook two or three cans at once, saving time and fuel. The boiled cans will store quite well until you want to use them.

2 Remove the saucepan from the heat and lift out the can, remembering that it will be hot. Leave it to cool at room temperature. Do **not** open the can when it is hot, or you will decorate your ceiling with caramel! When the can is quite cold, open with a tin-opener. You will find the condensed milk has transformed into a thick, golden caramel.

3 Slice the peeled bananas quite thickly and arrange over the base of the flan case. Then spread the caramel over the bananas as evenly as you can.

4 Finally, pour the cream into a bowl and whisk until it is quite thick. Spread this over the caramel. It looks nice with quite a rough finish, but ensure that all the caramel is covered.

5 Chill until required and then serve – to gasps of delight!

FRUITY LAYERS

It is a good idea to serve this dessert in wine glasses, so that you can see the layers.

Preparation time: 40 minutes + cooling

You will need:

700g (1¹/₂lb) fruit – rhubarb, apple, gooseberries and apricots all work well	275ml (10 fl oz) double cream
	Pinch of ground ginger, if using apples or rhubarb
110g (4oz) caster sugar	110g (4oz) gingernut biscuits

1 First prepare the fruit. Trim the leaf and root from the rhubarb and cut into 2.5cm (1 inch) lengths. Peel and core the apples and cut into thin slices. Top and tail the gooseberries (remove the remains of the stem and flower). Cut the apricots around the stone, then twist in half and remove the stone.

2 Place the fruit of your choice in a large pan with about 60ml (4tbspn) of water and the sugar. Cook over a low heat, stirring occasionally, until the fruit softens and becomes quite mushy. Remove the pan from the heat and allow the fruit to cool, then beat it with a wooden spoon until it becomes smooth.

3 Place half the cream in a bowl and whisk until it just stands in little peaks when you pull the whisk out.

4 Fold the fruit into the cream, adding the ground ginger if appropriate.

5 Crush the gingernuts by placing them in a plastic bag and attacking with a rolling pin or other heavy object. Be warned, gingernuts put up quite a fight, so you will need to be fairly vicious as you need quite fine crumbs.

6 Arrange alternate layers of fruit and biscuits in 4 wine glasses to give a stripy effect.

7 Place the other half of the cream in a bowl and whisk until thick. Place a spoonful on top of each glass. Chill for at least one hour before serving to allow the biscuits to soften slightly.

VARIATIONS

You could use a large can of fruit in natural juice instead of cooking your own.

Try amaretti biscuits (little Italian almond biscuits) instead of gingernuts.

CHOCOLATE BANANA CREAMS

Another quick and easy dessert that looks as if you spent ages preparing it. If you are serving it for a special occasion, you could add 15ml (1tbspn) brandy or rum to the mixture, but this is certainly not essential.

Preparation time: 30 minutes

You will need:
110g (4oz) good quality plain chocolate
150ml (5 fl oz) double cream
150ml (5 fl oz) single cream
2 large bananas, ripe but not brown and squishy

1 Break up the chocolate into squares and place in a bowl. Rest this bowl over a pan of boiling hot water and leave until the chocolate melts. As soon as this happens, lift the bowl off the water and allow to cool slightly.

2 In another bowl, place the two creams and beat together with a whisk until the cream stands in little peaks when you pull the whisk out.

3 Peel and roughly chop the bananas, then place them on a plate and mash with a fork or potato masher until they are fairly smooth.

4 Now simply mix the cream, chocolate and bananas together until well blended and spoon the mixture evenly into four small bowls or wine glasses. Chill for at least one hour before serving.

FRUIT FOOLS

These are some of the easiest cold desserts, since they involve only three or four ingredients and do not require any gelatine. If you serve them in tall-stemmed wine glasses, they look especially elegant.

Preparation time: 20 minutes

You will need:
450g (1lb) fresh fruit – strawberries, raspberries or peaches
275ml (10 fl oz) double cream
Icing sugar

1 Begin by pushing the fruit through a sieve resting over a bowl. To do this the fruit needs to be perfectly ripe. If you are using peaches, life is easier if you skin them. Cut the peaches in half and take out the stone. Place the fruit in a bowl and cover with boiling water. Leave for two minutes and then drain. You should find the skins slip away quite easily.

2 Place the cream in a bowl and whip with a whisk until it forms little peaks when the whisk is pulled out.

3 Now simply mix together the fruit and the cream, adding a little icing sugar to sweeten the mixture if you feel it needs it. With brightly coloured fruit such as raspberries, you can achieve a pretty effect by not mixing the cream and fruit too thoroughly.

4 Pile the fools into tall glasses or small bowls to serve.

VARIATIONS

You can, of course, use fruit that needs to be cooked to make a fool. Rhubarb and gooseberries are particularly good. Simply cut the rhubarb into 2.5cm (1 inch) pieces or top and tail the gooseberries (pinch off the remains of the flower and stalk). Place the fruit in a saucepan and add about 150ml (5 fl oz) of water. Bring to the boil over a high heat, then reduce the heat and simmer the fruit until tender. Then push the fruit through a sieve resting over a bowl, add sugar to taste and allow to cool. Proceed as for fresh fruit.

As an alternative to cream, you can use cold custard. Either make as directed on the packet and allow to cool, or buy a carton of the ready-made variety. Greek yoghurt and fromage frais can also be used partly or totally to replace the cream.

CHOCOLATE MOUSSE

This classic dessert is extremely rich, so don't worry if the portions seem small. The mousse looks good in small ramekin dishes but could be served in wine glasses. This recipe contains raw eggs, so don't offer it to young or elderly guests or anyone who might be pregnant.

Preparation time: 30 minutes + chilling

You will need:
50g (2oz) good quality plain chocolate per person (see Cook's tip)
1 egg, separated, per person (see page 68)

1 Half fill a saucepan with water and find a bowl that will sit over the saucepan with the base just touching the water. Bring the saucepan of water to the boil over a high heat, then reduce the heat until the water is barely bubbling.

2 Sit the bowl over the saucepan and add the chocolate, broken into squares. Leave for about 10 minutes, by which time the chocolate should be quite liquid. Remove from the heat.

3 Stir the egg yolks into the chocolate – don't worry that the mixture looks a little thick and dull.

4 In a large bowl, beat the egg whites until they are stiff. The test is that you should be able to turn the bowl upside-down and nothing slides out. A hand-held mixer does this very quickly, but a briskly used whisk comes a good second. Stir about 30ml (2tbspn) of the beaten egg white into the choco-late, which will soften the mixture and make it easier to add the rest of the egg whites.

5 Now add the rest of the egg whites and, using a metal spoon and folding movements (see page 69), combine the chocolate and egg whites very gently. Remember you are trying to hold in as much air as possible.

6 Pour the mixture into individual dishes and chill for about 2 hours or until firm.

7 You can top the mousses with a dollop of thick cream and serve with some elegant biscuits, but actually it is just as good on its own and people will never believe that you made it with just two ingredients.

Cook's Tip

Use good quality plain chocolate for this recipe. That sold as cooking chocolate or chocolate cake covering may be temptingly cheap but it isn't good enough – you need the real thing. Apart from anything else, you may need to eat up any you have spare!

FRUIT SALAD

If you have people to a meal and are not sure of their likes and dislikes, then fruit salad is a fairly safe bet for dessert. Some recipes include making syrup and dipping fruit in lemon juice to prevent browning. I have discovered that if you use a can of pineapple chunks in natural juice, you have your syrup and means to prevent browning quicker than you can say tin-opener. Just use more or less fruit depending on numbers.

Preparation time: 30 minutes

You will need:

Can of pineapple chunks in natural juice

Bananas

Apples – green and red skinned

Pears

Satsumas or similar

Seedless black and green grapes

Kiwi fruit

1 Drain the juice from the can of pineapple into your serving bowl.

2 Peel the bananas, cut into slices about 5mm ($1/4$ inch) thick and toss in the pineapple juice.

3 Wash the apples and pears but do not peel them. Cut into quarters and cut away the cores with a sharp knife. Then cut across each quarter to give slices about 5mm ($1/4$ inch) thick. Add to the bowl, stirring the pieces round in the pineapple juice to ensure that they are all coated.

4 Peel the satsumas and divide into segments, making sure you remove all the white stringy bits and any pips that are evident.

5 Wash the grapes and dry them on kitchen paper. Pull off the stalks. Add the grapes to the salad whole if small or halved if larger.

6 Peel the kiwi fruit, cut into thin slices and add to the bowl.

7 Mix the fruit together very gently, cover the bowl with film wrap and chill for at least 30 minutes before serving. Fruit salad is delicious served with pouring cream and shortbread or sponge-finger biscuits.

VARIATIONS

Obviously the above recipe is only a guide. At various times of the year, you could also add fresh strawberries, melon and peaches or nectarines, quartered, stoned and sliced.

For a touch of luxury, add 15ml (1tbspn) of fruit liqueur, such as apricot brandy or grand marnier, to the juice.

Try a green fruit salad for a difference. Use the pineapple as a base and add green-skinned apples and pears, green grapes, kiwi fruit and green-fleshed melon. You might consider adding a little freshly chopped mint.

HONEYCOMB MOUSSE

This dessert is so easy to make but tastes divine. Adjust the ratio of cream to yoghurt to suit your own taste. Serve and let your guests guess the ingredients!

Preparation time: 15 minutes + chilling

2 average-sized chocolate-covered honeycomb bars
275ml (10 fl oz) double cream
75ml (5tbspn) natural yoghurt – a rich, thick type, such as Greek yoghurt, is best
1 egg white

1 Begin by roughly breaking up the honeycomb bars by placing them in a plastic bag and attacking them with a rolling pin or other blunt instrument. Don't get too carried away – you want a majority of smallish chunks with a little powder.

2 Beat the egg white with a whisk until it is stiff. Beat the cream until it stands in soft peaks when the whisk is removed. Remember, if you tackle the egg white and cream this way round, you don't have to wash up your whisk between the two operations. Mix the yoghurt into the cream and then fold in the egg white as lightly as possible.

3 Carefully fold in the crushed honeycomb bars and divide the mixture between four dishes or glasses.

4 Chill for at least 2 hours before serving. You'll find that some of the honeycomb will start to melt and trickle through the mousse, while other pieces will retain their crunchy texture – delicious!

SYLLABUB

This makes a great dessert for a dinner party or other special meal. Remember you can always buy miniature or quarter bottles of sherry and brandy. This syllabub can be made a day in advance if you wish.

Preparation time: 20 minutes

1 large lemon
150ml (5 fl oz) sweet sherry
30ml (2tbspn) brandy

50g (2oz) caster sugar
275ml (10 fl oz) double cream

1 Grate the zest from the lemon on the finest side of your grater and then squeeze out the juice. Place both in a bowl with the sherry, brandy and sugar and stir until the sugar has dissolved.

2 Pour the cream into the lemon mixture and start whisking. If you have a hand-held electric mixer, so much the better, but a hand whisk will work well and you can feel less guilty eating this pudding, knowing how much energy you have expended! Eventually the mixture will be thick enough to form peaks when you take the whisk out.

3 Spoon the mixture into wine glasses or small bowls and chill until required. This is good served with shortbread (see page 207), especially if you add the zest of one lemon to the short-bread mixture before baking.

CHOCOLATE AND CHESTNUT LOAF

This rich, chocolate dessert is bound to please any pudding lover. I think it is especially nice at Christmas time, served with whipped cream. It can be made two or three days in advance and certainly needs to be chilled overnight. A loaf tin makes it easy to slice, but it can be made in any shaped mould or even divided into small serving dishes.

Preparation time: 25 minutes + chilling

225g (8oz) good quality plain chocolate
90ml (6tbspn) water
450g (1lb) can unsweetened chestnut purée

75g (3oz) caster sugar
110g (4oz) butter, softened
2 eggs, separated

1 Place the chocolate and water in a pan over a very low heat. Stirring occasionally, heat until the chocolate has just melted and blended with the water. Remove from the heat.

2 Place the chestnut purée in a bowl and beat with a wooden spoon to make it fairly smooth – it is quite solid and needs breaking up. Add the butter and sugar and beat together well. Add the chcolate mixture and egg yolks and beat well until quite smooth, although a few lumps of chestnut purée are not a disaster.

3 In another bowl, beat the egg whites with a whisk until stiff. Fold these into the chestnut mixture until thoroughly mixed, being as light-handed as possible to retain all the air you can.

4 Turn the mixture into a lightly oiled tin, which has had the base lined with greaseproof paper, and refrigerate overnight.

5 To serve, run a knife around the edge of the tin and turn on to a serving plate. Peel off the greaseproof paper if it has stuck.

BAKING

RECIPES

CINNAMON AND ALMOND COOKIES

Crisp little biscuit squares, flavoured with ground cinnamon and sprinkled with flaked almonds.

SHORTBREAD

A classic biscuit, buttery, crisp and crumbly.

OATY COCONUT BISCUITS

Light and crunchy biscuits, easily made by melting and mixing.

GINGER BISCUITS

Delicious ginger biscuits, cooked to perfection when they have a slightly chewy centre.

CHEESE STRAWS

A classic savoury nibble, perfect at afternoon tea and delicious served with soup.

COFFEE SLICE

A rich and crunchy mixture for condensed-milk lovers everywhere.

CRUSTY LEMON BAKE

Light sponge cake coated with a crust of sugar and lemon juice.

LUCY'S CHOCOLATE FUDGE SLICES

Crushed biscuits, blended with golden syrup, butter and cocoa powder and topped with melted chocolate for a rich treat.

FLAPJACK

Slightly gooey but also slightly crispy, these little cakes are sure to be a favourite.

GINGERBREAD

A rich, dark and moist cake that actually improves with keeping, becoming even stickier.

GOLDEN CRISPIES

A favourite with children and their parents alike, puffed rice cereal is bound together with a toffee sauce.

CHOCOLATE APRICOT SLICE

A recipe that can be served warm as a dessert or cold as a cake.

BARM BRACK

A delicious teabread, unbelievably simple to make and a surprising use for cold tea.

SANDWICH CAKE

Use this basic recipe to make a classic Victoria sandwich, buns, finger cakes and pineapple upside-down cake.

PLAIN SCONES

At the heart of any good afternoon tea are scones, light, fluffy and warm from the oven.

POTATO CAKES

Serve these delicious and versatile little cakes warm, with butter and jam or eggs and bacon.

IRISH WHOLEMEAL BREAD

Made with soda rather than yeast, this bread is simple to make but crusty and delicious to eat.

CINNAMON AND ALMOND COOKIES

This is a particularly easy recipe because it is made in a slab and then cut up and so does not involve a lot of rolling out and cutting of shapes.

Makes: 18 pieces
Preparation time: 20 minutes
Cooking time: 20 minutes

You will need:

Vegetable oil
110g (4oz) butter, at room temperature
50g (2oz) caster sugar
170g (6oz) plain flour

2.5ml (1/2tspn) ground cinnamon
Milk
25g (1oz) flaked almonds
15ml (1tbspn) granulated sugar

1 Brush a 30 x 20cm (12 x 8 inch) shallow rectangular tin with vegetable oil.

2 Place the butter and sugar in a bowl and beat together with a wooden spoon until light and fluffy. Sift in the flour and cinnamon and work together, with the spoon or your hands, whichever you find easiest, to give a rough dough.

3 Press the dough into the prepared tin, using your knuckles to spread it out evenly. When you have got it up to the edges of the tin and into all the corners, press the dough with the palm of your hand to give a smooth surface. Brush the top with a little milk and sprinkle over the nuts and granulated sugar as evenly as possible.

4 Bake in an oven preheated to 180°C/350°F/Gas Mark 4 for 20 minutes, until golden brown. Cut into three widthways and six lengthways to make 18 fingers, but leave in the tin until fairly cool and crisp. Remove with a palette knife and finish cooling on a wire rack. Store in an airtight tin when completely cold.

SHORTBREAD

Although there are many shortbreads available on the super-market shelves, some of very good quality, they cannot compete with the homemade variety. Remember, it is called shortbread because of its short and crumbly texture, so try not to handle the dough too much.

Makes: 8 wedges
Preparation time: 15 minutes
Cooking time: 45 minutes

You will need:
175g (6oz) plain flour
50g (2oz) caster sugar + extra for dusting
110g (4oz) butter, cut into small pieces

1 Sift the flour into a bowl. Mix in the sugar and add the butter.

2 With your fingers, work the butter into the flour and sugar until the mixture begins to come together to form a dough.

3 Turn out on to a floured work-surface and knead very lightly to smooth the dough. Shape into a circle about 17.5cm (7 inches) across and pinch around the edges to make a pattern.

4 Slide the shortbread on to a baking tray and lightly mark into 8 wedges, not cutting all the way through the dough.

5 Bake at 170°C/325°F/Gas Mark 3 for about 45 minutes, until firm and golden brown.

6 Remove from the oven, cut into wedges where you previously marked, this time going through to the baking tray, and sprinkle lightly with caster sugar while still hot. Cool on the baking tray and then transfer to a wire rack to finish cooling.

OATY COCONUT BISCUITS

These are light and crunchy biscuits, quickly prepared by melting and mixing. They make a good accompaniment to stewed fruit or ice-cream, as well as being delicious on their own. If you have only one baking tray, you will need to cook the biscuits in batches.

Makes: about 30 biscuits
Preparation time: 15 minutes
Cooking time: 20 minutes

You will need:

50g (2oz) golden syrup (see Cook's tip)
150g (5oz) margarine
110g (4oz) caster sugar
75g (3oz) rolled oats

50g (2oz) desiccated coconut
110g (4oz) plain flour
10ml (2tspn) bicarbonate of soda
Vegetable oil

1 Melt together the syrup, margarine and sugar in a large saucepan over a very low heat, stirring occasionally, until the margarine is liquid.

2 Remove the pan from the heat and use it as your mixing bowl. Add the oats, coconut and flour, and mix well.

3 Mix the bicarbonate of soda with 5ml (1tspn) of hot water in a small bowl or cup, add to the saucepan and mix well.

4 Take pieces of the mixture about the size of a table-tennis ball, roll into balls, place on a lightly oiled baking tray and press to flatten to about half their original thickness. They should be about 10cm (4 inches) apart to allow for spreading.

5 Bake in an oven preheated to 170°C/325°F/Gas Mark 3 for 20 minutes. Remove the tray from the oven and allow the biscuits to stand for 2 minutes until they just start to harden. Remove from the tray with a palette knife or fish slice and cool on a wire rack. Store in an airtight container when totally cold.

Cook's Tip

When weighing golden syrup, it is easiest to stand the can of syrup on the scales, calculate the end weight when you have removed the required amount, then take out the syrup with a spoon, allowing any excess to trickle back into the tin until the required weight is achieved.

GINGER BISCUITS

These are really easy to make and the trick here is to slightly undercook them. This way they are crispy round the outside and slightly chewy in the middle. You can adjust the ginger level in this recipe to your taste. The amount given results in a fairly mildly flavoured biscuit.

Makes: 30–40 biscuits
Preparation time: 10 minutes
Cooking time: about 10 minutes

You will need:

225g (8oz) self-raising flour
5ml (1tspn) ground ginger
110g (4oz) soft brown sugar

75g (3oz) margarine
110g (4oz) golden syrup
Vegetable oil

1 Sift together the flour and the ginger.

2 In a large pan, melt together the margarine and syrup until just liquid. Remove from the heat.

3 Mix the flour, ginger and sugar into the syrup mixture to make a thick paste.

4 Roll out the biscuit mixture on a well-floured worktop to about 3mm (^{1}/$_8$ inch) thick. Cut out shapes with a biscuit cutter or the top of a glass and place on a lightly greased baking tray. The mixture hardly spreads, so the shapes can be quite close together. Re-roll the trimmings as necessary.

5 Bake at 190°C/375°F/Gas Mark 5 for about 10 minutes, until the edges are starting to tinge a darker brown. Allow to cool on the tray for a minute, then lift off with a palette knife or fish slice and cool on a wire rack. Allow the biscuits to get quite cold before storing in an airtight container.

CHEESE STRAWS

The temptation at tea parties is to serve scones, cakes and biscuits, but these classic little savoury nibbles provide a some-times welcome break from the sweet things. They are also quite delicious served with soup.

Makes: lots!
Preparation time: 20 minutes
Cooking time: 10 minutes

You will need:

175g (6oz) plain flour
2.5ml (^{1}/$_2$tspn) mustard powder
2.5ml (^{1}/$_2$tspn) salt
75g (3oz) butter
75g (3oz) strong cheddar cheese, grated finely

Cold water to mix
1 egg, beaten
Vegetable oil

1 Sift the flour, mustard powder and salt into a mixing bowl. Add the butter, cut into small pieces. Rub the fat into the flour until there are no lumps left.

2 Stir in the cheese and add the water, a little at a time, until the mixture starts to form a dough. Turn out on to a work-surface and knead very gently until the mixture forms a smooth ball.

3 Roll out the pastry on a floured work-surface to a rectangular shape about 5mm (1/4 inch) thick. Trim into strips about 7.5cm (3 inches) wide and as long as you can get from your pastry. Re-roll the left-over pastry and repeat this stage.

4 Brush the tops of the pastry strips lightly with the beaten egg, then take a sharp knife and cut across the strips to make fingers about 5–10mm (1/4–1/2 inch) wide.

5 Using a palette knife or fish slice, lift these on to a lightly oiled baking tray and spread out lightly to leave a small space between each finger.

6 Bake in an oven preheated to 200°C/400°F/Gas Mark 6 for about 10 minutes until golden brown. Remove from the tray straightaway or the cheese that may have bubbled out will weld them to the tray as it cools. It is the cook's perk to nibble a few of these warm from the oven!

COFFEE SLICE

If you have a sweet tooth, you will love this recipe, which involves no cooking.

Makes: 24 pieces
Preparation time: 20 minutes

You will need:

275g (10oz) semi-sweet biscuits such as
    digestive, rich tea or shortbread
110g (4oz) butter
1 large tin condensed milk

15ml (1tbspn) instant coffee
175g (6oz) icing sugar
110g (4oz) plain chocolate

1 Place the biscuits in a plastic bag and crush with a rolling pin or similar heavy object. Leave some pieces – you do not want to reduce them to a powder.

2 Melt the butter, condensed milk, coffee and sugar in a large pan over a low heat until the butter is liquid. Add the biscuits and mix well.

3 Press the mixture into a 30 x 20cm (12 x 8 inch) shallow tin, spreading it out evenly and pressing it down well.

4 Melt the chocolate (see page 194) and pour over the biscuit base, spreading it evenly right to the corners and edges. Leave to set, then cut into squares and lever out of the tin with the aid of a palette knife.

CRUSTY LEMON BAKE

This is an excellent cake because, although it has the texture of a light sponge, it is simply made by melting and mixing in a saucepan, with no tedious beating involved. Everybody loves the sharp yet crunchy topping on this cake, and you could vary it by using the juice of half an orange or two limes instead.

Makes: 16 pieces
Preparation time: 15 minutes
Cooking time: 40 minutes

You will need:

175g (6oz) margarine
175g (6oz) light soft brown sugar
2 eggs
175g (6oz) self-raising flour

110g (4oz) caster sugar
Juice of 1 large lemon (see Cook's tip)
Vegetable oil and greaseproof paper

1 Melt the butter in a large pan over a very low heat.

2 Remove the pan from the heat and stir in the eggs and brown sugar. Beat in the flour, until the ingredients are well blended.

3 Line the base of a 30 x 20cm (12 x 8 inch) tin with grease-proof paper and brush lightly with oil. Pour the mixture into the tin and spread it out evenly to cover the base.

4 Bake in an oven preheated to 180°C/350°F/Gas Mark 4 for about 40 minutes, until well risen and golden brown.

5 While the cake is cooking, mix together the lemon juice and caster sugar to make a thin paste. As soon as the cake comes out of the oven, pour the paste on to the cake and quickly spread it out evenly right to the corners and edges. Allow the cake to cool in the tin. The juice will sink into the cake and leave a sugary crust.

6 Cut into pieces with a sharp knife and remove from the tin using a palette knife. Store in an airtight tin.

Cook's Tip

If you have a lemon squeezer, fine. If not, cut the lemon in half and stab a fork into the flesh. Hold the fork in one hand and (over a bowl) squeeze the lemon with the other, twisting the fork to get out as much juice as possible. Pick out any pips and pith (white bits) but leave any little bits of flesh, as these add an extra zing to the topping.

LUCY'S CHOCOLATE FUDGE SLICE

An easy-to-produce recipe, using just the hob. Add toasted flaked almonds, chopped walnuts or chopped glacé cherries if you like.

Makes: 24 pieces
Preparation time: 15 minutes + setting

You will need:

225g (8oz) rich tea biscuits
225g (8oz) shortbread biscuits
30ml (2tbspn) golden syrup
15ml (1tbspn) cocoa powder

175g (6oz) butter
15ml (1tbspn) caster sugar
150g (5oz) plain chocolate

1 First crush the biscuits. This is best done by placing them in a plastic bag and attacking them with a rolling pin or similar object. For this recipe, it is nice to leave a bit of texture, so don't crush them to a powder.

2 Melt the syrup, butter and cocoa powder in a pan over a low heat. Chose a big enough pan so you can also do all your mixing in it.

3 Stir in the crushed biscuits, nuts and cherries (if using) and mix well until they are evenly covered.

4 Press the mixture into a 30 x 20cm (12 x 8 inch) tray, pushing it down well and evenly.

5 Melt the chocolate (see Cook's tip) and spread it evenly all over the top of the biscuit mixture. Leave to cool and set.

6 Cut the cake into about 24 squares and prise out of the tin with the aid of a palette knife. Once the first one or two pieces come out, the rest will be much easier to manage. Assuming you don't manage to eat it all in one session, store the cake in an airtight tin in a coolish place.

Cook's Tip

Melting chocolate. Break the chocolate up into squares and place in a small bowl. Boil up the kettle and pour the water into another, slightly larger, bowl. Now sit the bowl containing the chocolate inside the water-filled bowl (but make sure that the water does not come over the top) and the chocolate will quickly melt. If you have a microwave, place the chocolate in a bowl and heat it for 30 second bursts on full power, stirring gently in between, until the chocolate has melted.

Never attempt to melt chocolate in a pan directly on the hob and try not to get any water or steam in with the chocolate, as this will make it go thick and grainy, although it will still usually taste acceptable.

FLAPJACKS

There are countless flapjack recipes, some very gooey, others dry and crumbly; some with coconut, others with black treacle. In my opinion, this recipe combines the best aspects of all of these.

Makes: about 24 pieces
Preparation time: 10 minutes + cooling
Cooking time: 15 minutes

You will need:

175g (6oz) butter

25g (1oz) golden syrup

110g (4oz) soft brown sugar

175g (6oz) porridge oats

50g (2oz) desiccated coconut

50g (2oz) wholemeal flour

Vegetable oil

1 Place the butter and syrup in a pan over a low heat and melt together.

2 Remove the pan from the heat and stir in the remaining ingredients except the oil. Mix thoroughly.

3 Grease a 30 x 20cm (12 x 8 inch) shallow tin thoroughly with oil, then pour in the mixture and spread it out evenly right to the edges and corners.

4 Bake in an oven preheated to 180°C/350°F/Gas Mark 4 for 15 minutes. Allow to cool slightly in the tin before cutting the cake in half lengthways. Then cut across to make 2.5cm (1 inch) fingers. Cool a little more and then lever out of the tin with a palette knife and cool on a wire rack. You may have to sacrifice the first finger when getting flapjack out of the tin, but after the first one, it becomes much easier.

GINGERBREAD

Another easy-to-make, melt-together recipe, resulting in a dark and rich cake. If you prefer, you could replace the black treacle with more golden syrup.

Makes: 12 pieces
Preparation time: 15 minutes
Cooking time: 40 minutes

You will need:

Vegetable oil and greaseproof paper	110g (4oz) soft brown sugar
275g (10oz) plain flour	175g (6oz) black treacle
10ml (2tspn) ground ginger	175g (6oz) golden syrup
5ml (1tspn) bicarbonate of soda	2 eggs, beaten
110g (4oz) margarine	150ml (5 fl oz) hot water

1 Grease a 30 x 20 cm (12 x 8 inch) tin and line the base with greaseproof paper.

2 Sift the flour, ginger and bicarbonate of soda into a bowl.

3 In a large saucepan, melt together the margarine, sugar, black treacle and golden syrup over a low heat until they are just liquid. Add to the flour mixture with the eggs and water and mix everything together very thoroughly.

4 Pour the mixture into the prepared tin, level the surface with the back of a spoon, and bake in an oven preheated to 180°C/350°F/Gas Mark 4 for about 40 minutes, until the cake feels springy when you lightly press the top.

5 Cool in the tin for 10 minutes, then turn out on to a wire rack to finish cooling. Cut into squares to serve. Gingerbread keeps well in an airtight tin, if anything becoming stickier. Some would say it should be kept for two or three days before eatimg.

GOLDEN CRISPIES

These must be the easiest cakes to make as they do not require an oven and can be made in one pan. They are incredibly popular with children of all ages!

Makes: 12
Preparation time: 10 minutes

You will need:

75g (3oz) puffed rice cereal
60ml (4tbspn) golden syrup
15ml (1tbspn) caster sugar

15ml (1tbspn) butter
Few drops vanilla essence

1 Place the syrup, sugar and butter in a pan over a medium heat, stirring, until the sugar has dissolved and the butter melted. Increase the heat and bring the mixture to the boil. Boil for exactly one minute, stirring all the time.

2 Remove from the heat and stir in a couple of drops of vanilla essence. Add the puffed rice and mix well, until it is all evenly coated.

3 Arrange 12 bun cases on a tray and drop spoonfuls of the mixture into them until the mix is used up and the cases are evenly filled. Allow to cool and set before serving.

CHOCOLATE APRICOT SLICES

This is a versatile bake. You could serve it warm with cream or ice-cream as a dessert, but it is equally delicious cold with a cup of tea or coffee. It is made by the all-in-one method, so could not be easier.

Makes: 16 pieces
Preparation time: 15 minutes
Cooking time: 25 minutes

You will need:

Vegetable oil
110g (4oz) margarine at room
    temperature
110g (4oz) soft brown sugar
45ml (3tbspn) golden syrup
2 eggs

200g (7oz) self-raising flour
25g (1oz) cocoa powder
225g (8oz) dried apricots, cut into small
    pieces
90ml (6tbspn) water
110g (4oz) plain chocolate

1 First brush a 30 x 20cm (12 x 8 inch) shallow tin with vegetable oil.

2 Place the margarine, sugar, syrup and eggs in a large bowl. Sift in the flour and cocoa powder. Now use a wooden spoon to mix the dry ingredients carefully together until blended. Then beat for 2 minutes until the mixture looks smooth and creamy. Stir in the chopped apricots and beat in the water.

3 Spoon the mixture into the prepared tin and spread out evenly, right to the corners.

4 Bake in an oven preheated to 200°C/400°F/Gas Mark 6 for 25 minutes, until well risen and springy to the touch.

5 Meanwhile, break the chocolate into pieces and place in a small bowl. Sit this over a pan of very hot water and leave until the chocolate melts.

6 When the cake is cooked, remove it from the oven and spread the melted chocolate roughly over the top. You are not trying to get a smooth finish, so do not worry if bits of the cake are not covered.

7 Cool in the tin. Then cut into 16 pieces and remove from the tin with the help of a palette knife. Store in an airtight tin.

BARM BRACK

This is a delicious teabread that is incredibly simple to make, keeps well and freezes if necessary. You can make it in a loaf tin or a round cake tin, but a well-greased casserole dish will work just as well. Remember, the fruit needs to be soaked overnight, so a little forethought is required.

Makes: 1 loaf
Preparation time: 10 minutes + soaking
Cooking time: 1³/₄ hours
Oven/Freezeable

425ml (15 fl oz) strained cold tea
350g (12oz) mixed dried fruit
200g (7oz) soft brown sugar

275g (10oz) self-raising flour
1 egg
Vegetable oil

1 Put the tea, dried fruit and sugar in a bowl, stir to dissolve the sugar and leave overnight.

2 Sift the flour into the tea mixture, add the egg and beat with a wooden spoon to ensure that everything is thoroughly mixed.

3 Use a pastry brush to thoroughly oil the sides and base of a 20cm (8 inch) round cake tin or 1kg (2lb) loaf tin. Pour in the mixture and level off the top with the back of a spoon.

4 Bake in an oven preheated to 180°C/350°F/Gas Mark 4 for 1³/4hours.

5 Leave to cool in the tin for 10 minutes, then run a knife around the edges, hold a cooling rack over the top of the tin and turn everything upside-down so that the barm brack tips out on to the rack. Cool until cold.

6 Serve sliced, spread with butter.

SANDWICH CAKE

This is a cake mixture that forms the base for so many recipes. I have included a number of variations after the basic recipe, but there are many more. Remember, the recipe can be scaled up or down in 50g (2oz) and 1 egg amounts.

Makes: 1 cake
Preparation time: 20 minutes
Cooking time: 20–25 minutes

You will need:

Vegetable oil and greaseproof paper

110g (4oz) margarine

110g (4oz) caster sugar

2 eggs

110g (4oz) self-raising flour, sifted

1 Grease the base and sides of two 15–17cm (6–7 inch) round or one 30 x 20cm (12 x 8 inch) rectangular tin with oil and line the base with greaseproof paper.

2 Place the margarine and sugar in a mixing bowl. Beat together with a wooden spoon until the mixture becomes light and fluffy. This is a phrase often used, but when you actually make the recipe you will see what it means – the mixture turns from golden to palest yellow and takes on a mousse-like texture. Leaving the margarine at room temperature for an hour or so before you start will make the job a lot easier.

3 Break the eggs into a small bowl and beat them together with a fork. Add a trickle of egg to your margarine mixture and beat well, repeating this until all the egg is used. If you add the egg too quickly, the mixture will curdle. This is not a disaster, but you will loose some of the lightness of your cake.

4 Now put aside your wooden spoon. In stages 2 and 3, you could not be too vigorous, but this part requires a delicate touch. Add the flour to the bowl and fold it into the egg mixture using a large metal spoon. Folding means lifting and cutting the egg mixture around the flour and so gradually mixing it in. By using these cutting and folding motions, you will preserve the air you have worked so hard to incorporate. It may seem a slow process, but do not attempt to beat at this stage.

5 Spoon the mixture into your prepared tin(s), spreading it out evenly and making sure you take it right to the sides.

6 Bake in an oven preheated to 190°C/375°F/Gas Mark 5 for 20–25 minutes, until risen and golden brown. To test if it is cooked, press the centre of the cake lightly with your finger. If the cake is cooked, the small dent you have made should quickly spring back. If it does not, cook for a little longer and retest.

7 Run a knife around the edges of the cake, making sure you press it against the sides of the tin or you may cut into the cake. Lay a cooling rack over the top of the tin, turn everything upside-down and remove the tin. Leave the cake on the rack to cool.

8 When the cake is cool, cut it into two 20 x 15cm (8 x 6 inch) pieces if using a rectangular tin. Spread one half of the cake with jam – strawberry or apricot are the classic flavours, but you can use anything you have to hand – and top with the other half. Sprinkle a little caster sugar over the top for a professional finish.

CHOCOLATE CAKE

You will need:
Sandwich cake recipe (page 221)
15ml (1tbspn) cocoa powder
Chocolate and hazlenut spread

Sift the cocoa powder with the flour and proceed as for the basic recipe. Sandwich the cooled cake with the spread.

LEMON CAKE

You will need:
Sandwich cake recipe (page 221)
Zest of 1 lemon
Lemon curd

Add the lemon zest when creaming the margarine and sugar. Sandwich the cooled cake with the lemon curd.

COFFEE CAKE

You will need:

Sandwich cake recipe (page 221)	**COFFEE BUTTER CREAM**
10ml (2tspn) instant coffee	50g (2oz) softened butter
10ml (2tspn) hot water	110g (4oz) icing sugar, sifted
	5ml (1tspn) instant coffee
	5ml (1tspn) hot water

Mix the instant coffee with the hot water. Fold into the mixture with the flour. Sandwich the cooled cake with coffee butter cream, made by beating together the butter, icing sugar and instant coffee mixed with the hot water again.

SMALL CAKES

You will need:
Sandwich cake recipe (page 221)
110g (4oz) icing sugar
Cold water

Bake the mixture in a rectangular tin, then cut in half and sandwich together with one of the fillings suggested the recipes above. Cut into fingers about 7.5 x 2.5cm (3 x 1 inch). Spread each finger with icing as follows. Sift the icing sugar into a bowl and very slowly add enough cold water to make a thick paste that just flows. You can flavour the icing by using orange or lemon juice instead of the water, or instant coffee powder or granules or cocoa powder mixed with hot water. You could also colour it, using small amounts of food colouring. Don't worry if the icing trickles down the sides, as this looks quite attractive. Of course, if it keeps trickling and forms a pool at the bottom, your icing is a little too runny, so scrape it back into the bowl and add some more sifted icing sugar. You can let your imagination run riot decorating the cakes. Glacé cherries, nuts, chocolate buttons and hundreds and thousands are a good starting point – have fun!

PINEAPPLE UPSIDE-DOWN CAKE

You will need:
Sandwich cake recipe (page 221)   Medium-sized tin pineapple rings
50g (2oz) butter   Few glacé cherries (optional)
50g (2oz) soft brown sugar

224

1 Use a rectangular tin, but instead of greasing and lining it, melt the butter in a small pan over a low heat and pour into the tin. Sprinkle it evenly with the soft brown sugar.

2 Drain the pineapple slices (there should be 6–8 rings) and arrange the rings over the butter and sugar. If you are feeling artistic, place a glacé cherry half, cut side up, in each hole.

3 Follow the main recipe and carefully spread the cake mixture over the pineapple, so that you do not disturb your pattern. Try to seal the cake mixture to the edges of the tin so that the butter mixture does not ooze out. Cook in an oven preheated to 190°C/375°F/Gas Mark 5 for 30 minutes, then turn out carefully. The pineapple sometimes sticks, but if this happens just scrape it up and place it back in the appropriate place on the cake.

PLAIN SCONES

A good scone is the start of any decent afternoon tea and this recipe is from the person who makes the best scones I've tasted – my mum! The basic recipe can be varied in a number of ways.

Makes: about 12 scones
Preparation time: 15 minutes
Cooking time: 15 minutes

You will need:

225g (8oz) plain flour
15ml (1tbspn) caster sugar
2.5ml (1/2tspn) bicarbonate of soda
5ml (1tspn) cream of tartar

Pinch of salt
50g (2oz) margarine
Milk to mix

1 Sift the flour, sugar, bicarbonate of soda, cream of tartar and salt into a mixing bowl.

2 Cut the margarine into small pieces and add to the bowl. Then rub the margarine and flour between your fingers until they are incorporated and no big lumps of margarine remain.

3 Add the milk a little at a time while stirring the mixture with a knife or spatula until a soft dough is formed. Try to be as gentle as possible as, if you knead the dough, your scones will be hard and heavy.

4 Turn the dough out on to a floured work-surface and roll out to about 2cm (³/₄ inch) thick. Cut into rounds about 3 cm (1¹/₄ inches) across, using a biscuit cutter if you have one or the top of a glass or cup if not.

5 Arrange the rounds on a baking tray and brush the top of each with a little milk.

6 Place the tray in an oven preheated to 220°C/425°F/Gas Mark 7 for 12–15 minutes, until well risen and golden brown. Using a palette knife or fish slice, transfer the scones to a cooling rack. Serve with butter, jam and cream – this is no time to consider the calories!

VARIATIONS

Add 50g (2oz) of sultanas to the mixture after you have rubbed the margarine in.

Leave out the sugar and add 60g (2¹/₂oz) finely grated cheese and a pinch of mustard powder after you have rubbed the margarine in. A sprinkling of grated cheese on the tops, prior to baking, is attractive.

POTATO CAKES

These cakes are particularly good served warm with eggs and bacon or buttered and eaten with jam or marmalade. They are a good way of using up any left-over mashed potatoes and, because the recipe is in cup measures, you can adapt it to any quantities you have, using a tea cup or mug accordingly.

Makes: 8 cakes
Preparation time: 15 minutes, assuming
    you have ready-cooked potato
Cooking time: 25–30 minutes

You will need:

2 cups self-raising flour
40ml (2 heaped tbspn) softened butter
1¹/₂ cup mashed potato

Good pinch salt
¹/₄ cup milk

1 Sift the flour into a bowl and mix in the butter by rubbing it between your fingers as if you were making pastry, but it only has to be roughly mixed.

2 Add the potato and salt and mix well together.

3 Add the milk and, using your hands, mix it all together to make a soft dough.

4 Sprinkle some flour on to your worktop and scrape out the dough on to it. Roughly shape the dough into a round about 20cm (8 inches) across and 2cm (³/₄ inch) thick.

5 Transfer to a baking tray and cut into eight wedges with a sharp knife but do not pull the wedges apart (see the diagram on page 103).

6 Bake in an oven preheated to 220°C/425°F/Gas Mark 7 for 25–30 minutes, until golden brown.

IRISH WHOLEMEAL BREAD

This bread is delicious with soup or cheese and is best eaten fresh, within a day of making, or frozen until you need it. You should find buttermilk alongside cream in your supermarket.

Makes: 2 loaves
Preparation time: 15 minutes
Cooking time: 1¼ hours

You will need:

575g (1¼lb) wholemeal flour

110g (4oz) plain flour

125g (4½oz) margarine

15ml (1tbspn) bicarbonate of soda

15ml (1tbspn) salt

15ml (1tbspn) sugar

570ml (1pt) buttermilk or natural yoghurt

1 Sieve both the flours into a large bowl, tipping in any pieces of bran that may be left in the bottom of the sieve.

2 Add the margarine, cut into small pieces, and rub it into the flour between your fingertips until no lumps remain.

3 Mix the bicarbonate of soda with half the milk or yoghurt and quickly stir into the flour with the sugar and salt. Add the remaining milk or yoghurt and mix to a dough. Turn out on to a lightly floured worktop and knead gently until smooth .

4 Cut the dough in half and shape each piece into a round. Place on a baking tray and flatten the tops slightly by pressing with the palm of your hand. Using a sharp knife, cut a cross in the top of each loaf, each cut about 10cm (4 inches) long.

5 Bake in an oven preheated to 200°C/400°F/Gas Mark 6 for 1 hour, turn off the heat and leave in the oven for 15 minutes.

6 Cool the loaves on a wire rack, but not too much, as this bread is especially delicious served warm.

ENTERTAINING

Now that you are armed with a vast repertoire of recipes, it is time to think about entertaining. The following pages give some menu ideas for various occasions. Some of the recipes you will have already come across, others are new. But remember, these are just suggestions. You will have your own ideas and know your friends' tastes. Nothing is nicer than sharing a well-cooked meal, so be justly proud of what you have achieved.

MENUS

BRUNCH

A traditional late breakfast and early lunch combined that should certainly keep your guests going until teatime.

SUNDAY LUNCH

This is a great time to entertain but a heavy, traditional roast lunch can leave everybody unable to move all afternoon. This menu offers a lighter option, though equally delicious.

AFTERNOON TEA

The most civilized meal of all. Make sure nobody has a large lunch, so that they have room for all the goodies you have made!

DINNER PARTY

A menu designed to leave you as free as possible to enjoy the company of your guests.

BRUNCH

This is a great time to entertain. By combining breakfast and lunch, you only have to provide one meal and it can linger from about 10.00 am to mid-afternoon.

Sausages
Bacon
Scrambled eggs (page 83)
Tomatoes
Mushrooms
Sweetcorn fritters
Assortment of rolls
Butter
Assorted jams and honey
Help yourself muesli

The secret of this menu is to cook as many as possible of the hot dishes in the oven, which saves you juggling lots of pans and the grill. By baking the sausages, bacon, tomatoes and mushrooms, you will have time to concentrate on the sweetcorn fritters and scrambled eggs. I have suggested scrambled eggs because this is the easiest way to cook a lot of eggs at once. And if you are serving the brunch as a help-yourself buffet, then they are a lot easier to serve than fried eggs.

Brunch needs to be washed down with lots of tea and coffee, so it is probably a good idea to nominate a friend to be chief kettle-boiler, leaving you free to concentrate on the food.

OVEN-BAKED BREAKFAST

Serves: as many as you require
Preparation time: 30 minutes
Cooking time: 30 minutes

You will need:

Sausages – choose the thin ones that usually weigh about 1oz each, or 8 for 225g (8oz). Allow 2–3 per person.

Bacon – as you are making bacon rolls, choose rindless streaky bacon, smoked or unsmoked, and allow 3 rashers per person.

Mushrooms – choose evenly-sized mushrooms, about 4–5cm (1¹/₂–2 inches) across. Allow 4–5 per person.

Tomatoes – choose evenly-sized tomatoes, about the size of a golf ball. Allow 2 per person.

1 Cut between the sausages to separate them and place on a baking tray. They can be close, but ideally not touching. Prick each one with a knife two or three times.

2 Lay a rasher of bacon on a chopping board and slide along the length of it with the back of a knife to slightly stretch it. Then roll it up and slide it on to a cocktail stick. Repeat with the remaining rashers. You should be able to fit two or three rolls per cocktail stick. Lay them out on an ovenproof dish.

3 Trim the stalks on the mushrooms so that they are level with the edges of the caps and place them, stalk side up, on an ovenproof dish. Top each one with a little piece of butter and a sprinkling of salt and pepper.

4 Arrange the tomatoes, stalk end down, on an ovenproof dish. Cut a small cross in the top of each one and squeeze in a small piece of butter. Sprinkle with salt and pepper.

5 Preheat the oven to 200°C/400°F/Gas Mark 6. Cook in this order:

Place the sausages in the oven and cook for 10 minutes.

Add the bacon and tomatoes and cook for a further 10 minutes.

Add the mushrooms and cook for a further 10 minutes.

If your eggs and sweetcorn fritters are not quite ready by this time, turn the oven off, leave the door closed and everything will be fine for 10–15 minutes.

SWEETCORN FRITTERS

These are a memory of my childhood and to me no brunch would be complete without them. You may feel just as strongly about black pudding or baked beans, so adjust your menu accordingly.

Makes: about 20
Preparation time: 10 minutes
Cooking time: 20 minutes

⚃ V

You will need:

326g (11¹/₂oz) can sweetcorn kernels
1 egg
Pinch of salt and pepper

90g (3¹/₂oz) plain flour
Vegetable oil

1 Empty the can of sweetcorn with its juice into a bowl. Mix in the egg and salt and pepper. I find a fork is best tool for this.

2 Add the flour, a bit at a time, mixing well in between, until you have a mixture that drops gently from the fork.

3 Now heat 30ml (2tbspn) of oil in a pan over a medium to high heat. Drop spoonfuls of the mixture into the pan and spread out a little to give about 5cm (2 inch) rounds. Three or four fritters at one time is plenty to cope with. Cook the fritters for about 3 minutes, until bubbles are starting to break on the top surface, reducing the heat a little if the base appears to be getting too dark – it should be golden brown. Flip the fritters over with a palette knife or fish slice and cook for a further 2–3 minutes. Remove from the pan and repeat until all the mixture is used. Since you have the oven on, the grill cavity, if you have one, should be nice and warm. This makes a good spot to keep your cooked fritters while you are making the rest.

HELP-YOURSELF MUESLI

Supply a basic cereal mix and lots of little bowls of extras, and your guests can "customise" their muesli to their own taste.

Serves: 6–8
Preparation time: 10 minutes

225g (8oz) porridge oats
110g (4oz) wholewheat flakes
Pinch of salt

15ml (1tbspn) dried milk powder
110g (4oz) bran flakes

1 Simply mix everything together in a large bowl from which you can serve it, offering milk or yoghurt. Surround with small bowls of some or all of the following:

Soft brown sugar
Toasted hazelnuts

Toasted flaked almonds
Raisins

Red and green apples, cored and sliced and tossed in a little lemon juice
Bananas, peeled and sliced and tossed in a little lemon juice
Dried apricots, dates and figs, chopped if necessary

SUNDAY LUNCH

There is no law that says Sunday lunch has to be roast beef, Yorkshire pudding, roast potatoes, three vegetables and gravy. In fact, in these days of lighter eating, this might be off-putting for some people. The trickiest part of preparing such a meal is ensuring that all the various parts are cooked to perfection at exactly the same time. This is largely down to practice and knowing how long your hob takes to boil a pan of water. The following menu does away with a lot of the guesswork. If you are feeding children, it is a wise idea to serve a dessert with an ice-cream accompaniment. Then if the kids don't fancy the pudding, they can always tuck into the ice-cream and their parents do not feel obliged to force feed them.

Baked chicken parcels
Jacket potatoes (page 122)
Matchstick vegetables
German apple cake (page 185)
Vanilla ice-cream

BAKED CHICKEN PARCELS

The good thing about this recipe, apart from its taste, is the serious lack of washing up it produces. I have given quantities for one portion and you can simply scale it up to suit your numbers.

Preparation time: 10 minutes
Cooking time: 45 minutes

1 breast or leg chicken joint, about 200g (7oz)
2 mushrooms, thinly sliced
2 thin slices of onion

15ml (1tbspn) lemon juice
Salt and pepper
Foil

1 Cut a piece of foil about 30cm (12 inches) square

2 Place the chicken portion in the centre of the square and cover with the sliced mushrooms and onion slices. Add the lemon juice and a good sprinkling of salt and pepper.

3 Pull up the sides and corners of the foil to loosely encase the chicken and twist together at the top. All the ingredients should be sealed into the foil but there should be a gap between them.

4 Place the parcel on a baking tray in an oven, which should already contain your potatoes, preheated to 200°C/400°F/Gas Mark 6 for 35–40 minutes. Then remove, open up the foil a little to expose the top of the chicken, and return to the oven for a further 10 minutes.

5 Dish up carefully, actually unwrapping the foil on the plate so that you serve up all the juices.

VARIATIONS

You could add a sprig of tarragon, a whole clove of garlic, 5ml (1tspn) of pesto or a few chopped walnuts to the parcel, or you could add a couple of slices of eating apple and replace the lemon juice with cider.

MATCHSTICK VEGETABLES

I discovered these when I first cooked Christmas lunch for the whole family. I wanted to impress with an array of vegetables but did not have room on the hob. This is an easy way to cook four vegetables at once. The time is taken in the preparation, but you can do this well in advance and store the matchstick vegetables in a sealed plastic bag in the fridge. Put the saucepan of water on to boil just before you open up the foil on your chicken parcels.

Preparation time: 30 minutes
Cooking time: 6–8 minutes

You will need:

4 sticks of celery	Salt
3 medium sized carrots	Butter
1 leek	Ground black pepper
2 medium sized courgettes	

1 First prepare the vegetables. Trim the top and bottom of the celery stalks. Peel the carrots and trim the top and root. Trim the root and leaves of the leek, slit down the middle and wash thoroughly. Trim the top and bottom of the courgettes but do not peel.

2 Now cut each vegetable into pieces about 4cm (1^1/$_2$ inches) long. Cut these pieces into slices about 5mm (^{1}/$_4$ inch) thick and then cut across these slices to make matchstick-shaped pieces.

3 Place a large pan of water with 2.5ml (^{1}/$_2$tspn) salt added on a high heat and bring to the boil. Add the vegetables and return to the boil. Reduce the heat and simmer for 6–8 minutes, depending on your slicing skills and how you like your vegetables. Ideally they should still retain a little crunch.

4 Drain well and place in a serving dish. Top with a knob of butter and a good sprinkling of black pepper.

AFTERNOON TEA

This has to be my favourite meal – it is such a civilised way to entertain. Do not worry if you don't have a dainty teaset. Just treat yourself to a packet of the pretty paper napkins that are now available. Rather surprisingly, garden centres usually have a good choice of these. Fold them into triangles and place on a small plate with a knife for each guest. You can also use them to cover plates for the food. It is tempting to serve all sweet food, but balance this with some savoury nibbles. People like to hover between sweet and savoury – it usually means they can eat more!

Elegant sandwiches
Buttered scones (page 225)
Jam and whipped cream
Cheese straws (page 210)
Crusty lemon bake (page 213)
All-in-one chocolate cake and frosting

ELEGANT SANDWICHES

It may seem odd to be giving a recipe for sandwiches, but a badly made one is a sad thing. Cutting the crusts off may seem a waste of time and money, but the resulting sandwiches look so delicate that I am sure you will agree it is worth giving the birds a treat.

Makes: 24 sandwiches
Preparation time: 35–40 minutes

You will need:

1 sliced loaf, preferably the square "sandwich" type	Half a cucumber
Butter at room temperature	3 eggs
185g (6¹/₂oz) can pink salmon	45ml (3tbspn) mayonnaise
Salt and pepper	Salt and pepper
15ml (1tbspn) vinegar	Small punnet of cress

1 First prepare the fillings. Drain the salmon and place it in a bowl, picking out any skin and large bones. Small bones will disappear when you break up the fish. Now use a fork to mash the salmon. Add a good pinch of salt and pepper and the vinegar and mix well.

2 Run a potato-peeler down the sides of the cucumber to remove most of the skin. Cut the cucumber across into thin slices.

3 Bring a small pan, half filled with water, to the boil over a high heat. Gently lower in the eggs, one by one, on a spoon. Reduce the heat slightly so that the water bubbles gently and cook the eggs for 10 minutes. Quickly remove the pan from the heat, drain off the hot water and replace it with cold. Leave for a few minutes, then drain off the water and replace with more cold water. Repeat until the eggs are quite cold, then crack the shells and peel them off.

4 Place the eggs in a bowl and mash them with a fork until they are reduced to small, evenly-sized pieces. Add the mayonnaise and a good pinch of salt and pepper and mix thoroughly.

5 Using a pair of scissors, cut off the cress level with the top of the tub. Rinse in a sieve with cold water and pat dry on kitchen paper.

6 Now assemble the sandwiches. Discard the crusts and remove the next two slices of bread from the bag. Lay them on your work-surface so that they are mirror images – this ensures that the base and lid of the sandwich fit exactly. Repeat until you have six "pairs" of slices in front of you. Butter each slice, making sure to spread the butter right to the edges and corners of the bread.

7 Divide the salmon between three slices and spread out evenly. Cover well with cucumber slices and top with the appropriate lid.

8 Divide the egg mayonnaise between three slices of bread, sprinkle evenly with the cress and top each slice with its lid. You may find this is quite a generous amount of filling and you could stretch it to a further round if you wish.

9 Stack the three salmon sandwiches on top of each other on a chopping board, lining up the edges carefully. Now, using a bread knife, slice away the crusts on all four sides, cutting away as little as possible. Cut the pile of sandwiches into four triangles by slicing from corner to corner.

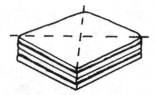 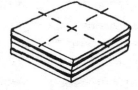

10 Stack and trim the egg sandwiches in the same way but work carefully because the filling is a little bit squishy. Cut into squares.

11 Arrange the sandwiches on a plate, cover with film wrap and leave in a cool place until required.

ALL-IN-ONE CHOCOLATE CAKE AND FROSTING

This is a really quick recipe. After all, every self-respecting afternoon tea needs a chocolate cake. Because it is an all-in-one mix and you do not do a lot of beating to incorporate air, you have to use self-raising flour and baking powder to make the cake light.

Makes: 1 cake
Preparation time: 20 minutes + cooling
Cooking time: 25 minutes

You will need:

Vegetable oil and greaseproof paper
170g (6oz) self-raising flour
7.5ml (1¹/₂tspn) baking powder
170g (6oz) soft margarine
170g (6oz) soft brown sugar
30ml (2tbspn) cocoa powder
30ml (2tbspn) boiling water
3 eggs

FROSTING

110g (4oz) plain chocolate
50g (2oz) butter
170g (6oz) icing sugar

1 Lightly oil a 30 x 20cm (12 x 8 inch) shallow rectangular baking tin and line the base with greaseproof paper.

2 Sift the flour and baking powder into a large mixing bowl and add the margarine, sugar and eggs. Mix the cocoa powder and water to a paste in a small bowl or cup and scrape into the mixing bowl. Mix gently with a wooden spoon until the ingredients are roughly combined. Now beat vigorously for 2 minutes, until the mixture is smooth and creamy.

3 Scrape the mixture into the prepared tin and spread out evenly, right to the edges. Place in an oven preheated to 180°C/350°F/Gas Mark 4 for 25 minutes, until the cake is well risen and feels springy when you press it gently in the middle.

4 Remove the cake from the oven, carefully run a knife around the edge of the tin to loosen the cake, and turn it out on to a wire rack to cool. When cold, cut in half to make two pieces 15 x 20cm (6 x 8 inches).

5 When the cake is quite cold, make the frosting. Do not be tempted to do this in advance, as it sets like fudge, and you want this to happen on the cake, not in your mixing bowl. Place the broken-up chocolate and the butter in a bowl and rest this over a pan of nearly boiling water. Leave until the butter and chocolate have melted. Remove the pan from the heat and sift in the icing sugar. Now beat well until the frosting starts to become thick and fudgy.

6 Spread some of the frosting over one piece of the cake and sandwich the other piece on top. Spoon the rest of the frosting over the top of the cake and swirl it about to make a pattern, allowing some to trickle down the sides of the cake. Leave to cool and store in an airtight tin until required.

DINNER PARTY

The thing to remember when planning a dinner party is that you are entertaining people! Therefore you do not want to be stuck in the kitchen all evening while everybody else is having a good time. This menu is designed so that the starter and pudding can be prepared well in advance, and most of the main course involves long, slow cooking, which can be prepared up to a point and then popped into the oven at the appropriate moment.

Smoked mackerel paté
Brown bread and butter

Beef in red wine
Potatoes O'Brien (page 128)
Braised red cabbage (page 129)
Cauliflower
Broccoli

Syllabub
Almond curls

SMOKED MACKEREL PATE

Fish is a good way to start a meal and this paté will freeze, so you can prepare it well in advance

Preparation time: 20 minutes + chilling

350g (12oz) smoked mackerel fillets	15ml (1tbspn) horseradish sauce
150ml (5 fl oz) soured cream	Salt and pepper
225g (8oz) low-fat soft cheese	1 lemon
Brown bread	Butter

1 Scrape the mackerel away from the skin and discard the skin. Remove any bones. Place the flesh in a bowl and add the soured cream, soft cheese and horseradish.

2 Beat everything together well to make a smooth, soft paté.

3 Add salt and pepper to taste and mix well. Pile the mixture into a bowl and chill for at least 1 hour in the fridge.

4 Butter the bread and cut across the diagonals to make small triangles. Cut the lemon in half lengthways and then in half again to make wedges.

5 To serve, place a large spoonful of the paté on a small plate for each guest, adding a lemon wedge and 4 triangles of bread and butter.

BEEF IN RED WINE

It is tempting when cooking with wine to use the cheapest variety possible, but remember that you only get out of a dish what you put into it. A decent red burgundy will be ideal for this dish. And bear in mind that the recipe only takes half a bottle, so it has got to be good enough to drink. You can make this dish up to three days in advance and keep it in the refrigerator. In fact, it could be argued that the dish actually mellows if you do so.

Preparation time: 50 minutes
Cooking time: 3¹/₄hours

You will need:

30ml (2tbspn) vegetable oil
900g (2lb) stewing beef – chuck steak is
    excellent for this dish
1 onion, peeled and thinly sliced
1 carrot, peeled and thinly sliced

20g (³/₄oz) plain flour
Half a bottle of red wine
150g (5 fl oz) beef stock
2 cloves garlic, crushed
Good pinch of salt and pepper

GARNISH

10ml (2tspn) vegetable oil

150g (5oz) streaky bacon

15 baby onions, peeled

150g (5oz) baby button mushrooms

15ml (1tbspn) chopped parsley

1 Cut the beef into 3cm (1^1/$_4$ inch) cubes, removing any large pieces of fat, but do not worry about trimming off every little spot of fat and gristle, as it will dissolve in the long, slow cooking.

2 Heat the oil in a large pan over a medium to high heat. Add about a quarter of the meat and toss around until browned on all sides. Transfer to a large casserole dish and repeat in batches until all the meat is browned and in the casserole.

3 Add the carrot and onion to the pan and fry, stirring, until tinged brown. Add the flour and cook, stirring, for 1 minute. Add the wine, garlic, stock, salt and pepper. Stir well until the mixture is boiling and then pour over the beef.

4 Place the casserole in an oven preheated to 170°C/325°F/Gas Mark 3 and cook for 3 hours, stirring occasionally. Add more stock if the mixture seems a little dry.

5 Meanwhile, prepare the garnish. Cut the bacon into strips about 1cm (^{1}/$_2$ inch) wide. Heat the oil in a pan over a high heat. Add the bacon and sizzle, stirring, until golden brown. Remove to a bowl. Add the onions and mushrooms to the pan and toss around until tinged brown. Place in the bowl with the bacon, cover and keep until required.

6 About 15 minutes before serving, stir the garnish into the casserole and return to the oven until required. Just before serving, sprinkle with the chopped parsley.

You will need to turn the oven up to 190°C/375°F/Gas Mark 5 for the last hour to cook the potatoes. When you add the garnish, you may want to add a little more stock if you think the casserole looks dry. The red cabbage will be quite happy at whatever temperature you have the oven.

When you add the garnish, put the saucepans of water on for the vegetables. Bring to the boil, add the vegetables, bring back to the boil, reduce the heat and simmer. Now summon your guests to the table for their first course. By the time they have finished it, your casserole and vegetables should be cooked to perfection.

ALMOND CURLS

An elegant, homemade biscuit improves any cold pudding. I have suggested a syllabub, but you could choose any other chilled fruity pudding mentioned in this book. If time is really short, simply serve the biscuits with one of the exotic ice-creams now available.

Makes: about 20 biscuits
Preparation time: 20 minutes
Cooking time: 8 minutes per batch

You will need:

75g (3oz) butter	50g (2oz) plain flour
75g (3oz) caster sugar	75g (3oz) flaked almonds

1 Place the butter and sugar in a bowl and cream together with a wooden spoon until softened and fluffy.

2 Sift the flour into the butter mixture, add the almonds and mix together to make a soft dough.

3 Scoop up teaspoonfuls of the mixture and place on a greased baking tray, leaving at least 5cm (2 inches) between each spoonful to allow room for spreading. Dampen a fork and press down on each mound of mixture with the back of the tines to flatten them out to about half their original height. Six biscuits per tray is as many as you will want to cope with at stage 5.

4 Bake the biscuits in an oven preheated to 200°C/400°F/Gas Mark 6 for 6–8 minutes, until well spread and tinged golden brown around the edges.

5 Remove the biscuits from the oven and leave for 1 minute. Now, working as quickly as you can, loosen around the edges of the biscuits with a palette knife, lift up the biscuits one at a time and drape over a rolling pin or wine bottle. The biscuits will quickly harden and take up the curled shape, when you can remove them to a cooling rack

6 Repeat with a further tray of biscuits until all the mixture is used up.

Cook's Tip

Reduce or increase the quantities depending upon how many guests you are serving. These biscuits are very brittle when cold, so handle them carefully. They can be made one or two days in advance and stored in an airtight tin.

INDEX

INDEX